Weight equivalents

IMPERIAL	METRIC	IMPERIAL	METRIC
$1/4$oz	10g	12oz	350g
$1/2$oz	15g	14oz	400g
$3/4$oz	20g	1lb	450g
scant 1oz	25g	1lb 2oz	500g
1oz	30g	$1^1/4$lb	550g
$1^1/2$oz	45g	1lb 5oz	600g
$1^3/4$oz	50g	$1^1/2$lb	675g
2oz	60g	1lb 10oz	750g
$2^1/2$oz	75g	$1^3/4$lb	800g
3oz	85g	2lb	900g
$3^1/2$oz	100g	$2^1/4$lb	1kg
4oz	115g	$2^1/2$lb	1.1kg
$4^1/2$oz	125g	$2^3/4$lb	1.25kg
5oz	140g	3lb	1.35kg
$5^1/2$oz	150g	3lb 3oz	1.5kg
6oz	175g	4lb	1.8kg
7oz	200g	$4^1/2$lb	2kg
8oz	225g	5lb	2.25kg
9oz	250g	$5^1/2$lb	2.5kg
10oz	300g	6lb	2.7kg

everyday easy
Cakes
& cupcakes

Based on content previously published
in *The Illustrated Kitchen Bible*
and *The Illustrated Quick Cook*

everyday easy

Cakes & cupcakes

cheesecakes • muffins
brownies • sponge cakes

DK

LONDON, NEW YORK, MELBOURNE, MUNICH, AND DELHI

US Editors Shannon Beatty, Beth Landis Hester

Editor Shashwati Tia Sarkar

Project Art Editors Elly King, Kathryn Wilding

Senior Jackets Creative Nicola Powling

Managing Editor Dawn Henderson

Managing Art Editor Marianne Markham

Senior Production Editor Jennifer Murray

Production Controller Poppy Newdick

DK INDIA

Editorial Manager Glenda Fernandes

Designer Neha Ahuja

Editor Alicia Ingty

Assistant Designer Nidhi Mehra

Assistant Editor Megha Gupta

DTP Coordinator Sunil Sharma

DTP Operator Saurabh Challariya

Material first published in *The Illustrated Kitchen Bible,* 2008
and *The Illustrated Quick Cook,* 2009
This edition first published in the United States in 2010
by DK Publishing, 375 Hudson Street
New York, New York 10014

10 11 12 13   10 9 8 7 6 5 4 3 2 1
178708—October 2010

A catalog record for this book is available
from the Library of Congress.

ISBN 978-0-7566-6731-3

DK books are available at special discounts when purchased in bulk
for sales promotions, premiums, fund-raising, or educational use.
For details, contact: DK Publishing Special Markets, 375 Hudson
Street, New York, New York 10014 or SpecialSales@dk.com.

Printed and bound in Singapore by Tien Wah Press

Discover more at
www.dk.com

CONTENTS

USEFUL INFORMATION 6
TECHNIQUES 8
RECIPE PLANNERS 20

SPONGE CAKES 30

FRUITY CAKES 62

LOAF CAKES 94

TRAYBAKES & SLICES 112

SMALL BAKES & MUFFINS 144

CUPCAKES 166

CHEESECAKES 190

MERINGUE CAKES 208

INDEX 222
ACKNOWLEDGMENTS 224

Baking ingredients

Understanding your ingredients and how to use them will improve your baking. Always measure carefully and never mix metric and imperial measurements.

INGREDIENT	CHOOSE	USE
	BUTTER Both **salted** and **unsalted butter** can be used for baking. Unsalted butter is mostly preferred in this book, but it's all a matter of taste preference, and whether you are reducing the salt in your diet. The amount of salt in salted butter varies, so check the label. Salted butter will keep for longer if you keep it in a butter dish out of the refrigerator.	Salted or unsalted, for cakes and bakes. Use softened butter (at room temperature). This means plenty of air will be held by the fat as you mix, making your cake or bake lighter.
	SUGAR **Granulated sugar** is commonly used for cakes and bakes. **Light and dark brown sugars** are plain white sugar with added molasses. Superfine sugar is finely ground granulated sugar. Confectioner's is granulated sugar crushed into a fine powder—ideal for dusting. Turbinado is a coarse, light-golden raw sugar that has been steam-cleaned. Muscavado is an unrefined brown sugar with a strong molasses flavor.	Granulated sugar is most common for cakes and bakes. White and brown sugars are equally sweet but the molasses in brown sugar create a moister texture.
	BAKING POWDER This is a rising agent used in baking. It is a mixture of bicarbonate of soda and cream of tartar, a natural rising agent, and is different from **baking soda**, which doesn't contain cream of tartar. The two cannot be interchanged. Check the sell-by date of baking powder, since it won't be effective if used when it's old.	Cakes and cookies. If a recipe calls for self-rising flour and you don't have any, you can modify all-purpose flour by adding $1\frac{1}{2}$ tsp baking powder and $\frac{1}{8}$ tsp salt per cup.
	FLOUR **All-purpose flour** and **self-rising flour** are relatively low in gluten, unlike strong bread flour. There are many flours that are suitable for a wheat-free or gluten-free diet, such as **rice flour**, **chestnut flour**, and **potato flour**. If using, consult specialist recipes; they are not interchangeable with all-purpose flour.	All-purpose flour or self-rising flour, sifted, for cakes and bakes. Don't over-beat once flour has been added, since the gluten will strengthen and you'll get a tough texture.
	EGGS Choose **organic** and/or eggs from **free-range hens**; they will improve the flavor and quality of your finished cake.	Use at room temperature. If they are used cold from the refrigerator, they cool the butter down and the mixture can curdle.

Tools of the trade

Baking pans should be rigid and sturdy, so they don't buckle in the heat of the oven. A selection of sizes and shapes is useful. For making a 4-egg sponge cake, you will need two 8in (20cm) round pans. Loose-bottomed cake pans are great—they make turning the cake out a lot easier. A springform pan is useful for larger cakes or more fragile ones, such as baked cheesecake.

If you are switching your pans from square to round, go up 1in (2.5cm) in size. If your recipe calls for a round 7in (18cm) pan, you can use an 8in (20cm) square pan. And if switching the other way, from round to square, go down 1in (2.5cm).

Baking sheets should be rigid and sturdy, so they don't buckle in the heat. Have a selection without lips and with lips (jelly roll pans).

A wire rack is necessary for cooling all cakes and bakes. Choose a large one if you plan to do batch baking.

Paper liners line the pan for cupcakes and muffins for a neater result.

Parchment paper is a grease-proof, moisture-resistant paper that withstands normal oven heat. It is used for lining baking sheets and baking pans to prevent food from sticking.

A small collection of essential baking tools is all you need to start baking.

A guide to symbols

The recipes in this book are accompanied by symbols that alert you to important information.

 Tells you how many people the recipe serves, or how much is produced.

Indicates how much time you will need to prepare and cook a dish. Next to this symbol you will also find out if additional time is required for such things as chilling, soaking, or rising. Read the recipe to find out exactly how much extra time to allow.

This is especially important, as it alerts you to what has to be done before you can begin to cook the recipe, or to parts of the recipe that may take a long time to complete.

 This denotes that special equipment is required, such as a springform pans or skewers. Where possible, alternatives are given.

 This symbol accompanies freezing information.

Test eggs for freshness

Always check the best-before date on the box. Or you can use this simple test if you have thrown the box away and have eggs without a best-before date: immerse the egg in water and see if it rises. A stale egg contains much more air and less liquid than a fresh one, so it will float. Do not use a stale egg.

Fresh

Borderline

Stale

Separate eggs

Many recipes call for either yolks or whites. Smell cracked eggs before using to be sure that they are fresh, or use the floating test shown above.

1 Break the shell of an egg by tapping it against the rim of the bowl. Insert your fingers into the break, and gently pry the two halves apart.

2 Gently shift the yolk back and forth between the shell halves, allowing the white to separate and fall into the bowl. Take care to keep the yolk intact.

Whisk egg whites

For the best results, use a clean, dry glass or metal bowl and a wire whisk. The whites must be completely free of yolk, or any other contact with grease.

1 Place the egg whites in a clean bowl (here a copper bowl is used) and begin beating slowly, using a small range of motion.

2 Continue beating steadily, using larger strokes, until the whites have lost their translucency, and begin to foam.

3 Incorporating as much air as possible, increase your speed and range of motion, until the whites are the desired volume, and are stiff, but not dry.

4 Test by lifting the whisk; the peaks should be firm but glossy, and the tips should droop gently.

Make sponge cake

This method will produce light, buttery sponge. Use two 8in (20cm) baking pans to make 2 sponges, which you can fill with fruit or cream if you like.

1 Preheat the oven to 350°F (180°C). In a bowl, cream together 1 cup softened butter with 1 cup granulated sugar, using an electric mixer or wooden spoon, until pale and fluffy.

2 Lightly beat 4 room-temperature eggs. Add them little by little to the butter and sugar, beating well. Add 1 tbsp sifted flour, taken from 2 cups self-rising flour, to prevent curdling.

3 Once all the egg is added, use a metal spoon to fold in the rest of the flour. The batter should drop off the spoon easily when it's ready. Add 1 tbsp of water if the mixture is too thick.

4 Divide the mix between 2 pans, and smooth out. Bake for 20 minutes, or until the cakes are risen and golden, and feel springy to the touch. Allow to cool slightly in the pans before turning out.

Prepare and line a baking pan

Greasing, flouring, or lining your pan not only ensures that baked layers turn out cleanly and easily, but will also care for your pans and help them last.

1 Melt unsalted butter (unless your recipe states otherwise), and use a pastry brush to apply a thin, even layer over the bottom and sides of the pan, making sure to brush butter into the corners.

2 Sprinkle a small amount of flour into the pan. Shake the pan so the flour coats the bottom, and rotate the pan to coat the sides. Turn the pan upside down and tap to remove the excess flour.

3 Or, to line with parchment paper instead of flour, stand the pan on the parchment and draw around the base with a pencil. Cut out the shape just inside the pencil line.

4 Place the piece of parchment paper directly on the bottom of the greased pan. This layer of parchment can be peeled off the bottom of your cake once it is baked and cooled.

Make cheesecake

This simple, basic recipe for a no-cook chilled cheesecake can be adapted by adding your own fruit and flavors. It makes an 8in (20cm) cheesecake.

1 Process 9oz (250g) graham crackers in a food processor, or place in a plastic bag and crush with a rolling pin. Melt 10 tbsp butter and stir in the crumbs. Spoon into a round springform pan, and spread the mixture evenly and firmly into the base.

2 Put 3 tsp powdered gelatin into a glass bowl with the juice of 3–4 lemons. Stir in 1 tsp water, and place the bowl over a pan of simmering water. Stir until the gelatin dissolves. Add $1/4$ cup sugar, and continue stirring until the sugar dissolves.

3 Make the topping by lightly whisking $1^3/_4$ cups heavy cream, then adding 8oz (225g) mascarpone, and 9oz (250g) cream cheese. Add a couple of drops of vanilla extract, then pour in the gelatin mixture. Stir well to combine.

4 Pour the batter over the base, and smooth the top. To set, put in the refrigerator for about 2 hours, or overnight if you prefer. Make sure it is completely set before releasing it from the pan Decorate with berries of your choice to serve.

Make a jelly roll

A jelly roll is less likely to tear if filled and rolled up while it is still warm and flexible. Take care not to overfill before rolling it, too.

1 Carefully line a jelly roll pan with a fitted piece of parchment paper. Make the mixture for the sponge cake, taking care to fold in the egg white mixture very gently, so that none of the volume is lost.

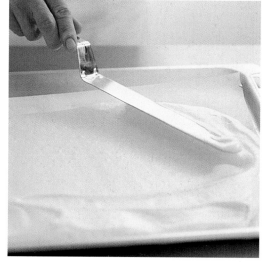

2 Spread the batter evenly in the lined jelly roll pan, using a spatula. Bake until golden and springy to the touch. Sprinkle with a little sugar, and cover with a clean piece of parchment paper. Carefully turn the cake out face down onto a work surface.

3 Slowly peel away the top (old) lining paper, pressing down onto it with a ruler to avoid tearing the cake. Spread with your desired filling. Lifting the cake with the help of the new piece of parchment paper underneath, roll it up with gentle pressure.

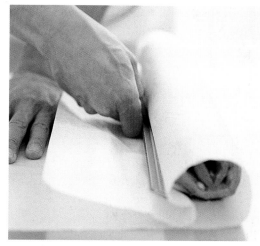

4 Drape one half of the paper over the roll. Hold the other end of the paper with one hand, and push a ruler against the roll with your free hand. This will tighten and shape the roll evenly. Remove the paper, refrigerate, and trim the ends to serve.

Whip cream

You can whip cream to soft or stiff peaks. Chill the cream beforehand and put the cream in a bowl set over a large bowl of ice before whipping.

1 Start beating in broad circles at about 2 strokes per second (or the lowest speed on a handheld electric mixer), until the cream begins to thicken.

2 Increase to a moderate speed for soft peaks. Lift the whisk to test—the cream should just retain its shape. Stiff peaks will retain their shape easily.

Pipe

A pastry bag can be used to pipe whipped cream, and also buttercream, meringue, and choux pastry.

1 Place the nozzle in the bag and twist to seal. Holding the bag just above the nozzle with one hand, fold the top of the bag over to create a "collar," and begin spooning in the filling.

2 Twist the top of the bag to clear any air pockets. Holding the twisted end taut in one hand, use your other hand to gently press the filling to start a steady flow, and direct the nozzle as desired.

Prepare chocolate

Chill the chocolate before cutting and grating, since the warmth of your hands will quickly melt it.

For chopping, break the chocolate into small pieces, then chill the pieces in the freezer for a few minutes. Place on a cutting board and use a sharp knife to chop into fine pieces using a rocking motion.

For grating, rub chilled chocolate against the face of the grater, using the widest holes. If the chocolate begins to melt, put it back in the freezer and continue grating once it has re-hardened.

To melt chocolate, break it into pieces and place in a heatproof bowl set over a pan of gently simmering water. Allow the chocolate to melt, then stir with a wooden spoon until smooth.

For curls, spread softened or melted chocolate onto a cool marble surface. When it solidifies, use the blade of a chef's knife to scrape the chocolate into curls.

Rich vanilla buttercream frosting

This simple recipe can be used to frost cupcakes and to sandwich cake layers together. You could add a few drops of food coloring, if you wish.

INGREDIENTS

$1/2$ cup butter, at room temperature

3 tbsp whole milk, as needed

1 tsp pure vanilla extract

$31/2$ cups confectioner's sugar

METHOD

1 Place the butter, 2 tbsp milk, and the vanilla extract in a large mixing bowl and beat with an electric mixer until smooth.

2 With the mixer on low speed, gradually add the confectioner's sugar, beating until the frosting is spreadable. If the frosting is too stiff, add the remaining milk.

PREPARE AHEAD The buttercream frosting can be refrigerated in a covered container for 2 days. Bring to room temperature before using. If too stiff to spread, stir in a little extra milk.

makes almost 2 cups

prep 10 mins

electric mixer

Crème pâtissière

This sweet pastry cream is great for European-style cakes and desserts.

INGREDIENTS
1¼ cups whole milk
2 large egg yolks
¼ cup sugar
2 tbsp all-purpose flour
2 tbsp cornstarch
¼ tsp pure vanilla extract

METHOD
1 Bring the milk to a simmer in a saucepan over medium heat.

2 Whisk the yolks and sugar together in a bowl. Whisk in the flour and cornstarch. Gradually whisk in the hot milk.

3 Return the mixture to the saucepan. Cook over medium-low heat, whisking constantly, until it comes to a full boil and is smooth.

4 Let cool slightly, then stir in the vanilla. If not using immediately, cover with a piece of buttered parchment paper pressed directly onto the surface of the pastry cream.

PREPARE AHEAD The pastry cream can be refrigerated, with parchment paper pressed on its surface, for up to 2 days.

makes about
1¼ cups

prep 10 mins
• cook 5 mins

Celebration

Blueberry and pistachio angel cupcakes page 184

All-in-one chocolate cake with fudge frosting page 46

Toffee-topped banana cake page 90

Black Forest gâteau page 92

Bienenstich page 44

Orange and lemon cupcakes page 172

Tropical angel cake page 84

Apple fruitcake page 86

Vanilla cupcakes page 168

Chocolate roulade page 48

Coconut and lime cake
page 80

Sachertorte page 52

Great for kids

Strawberry and cream cupcakes page 182

Chocolate cookie torte page 142

Apple muffins page 160

Sticky toffee shortbread page 124

Petit fours page 152

Madeleines page 146

White chocolate and macadamia nut blondies page 116

Orange and lemon cupcakes page 172

Banana and chocolate chip muffins page 158

Sticky date bar cookies
page 122

Chocolate-frosted cupcakes page 170

Cherry and coconut cupcakes page 186

Mini banana and chocolate cheesecakes page 206

Chocolate and buttercream Swiss roll page 42

Quick

Nutty date muffins page 150

Swiss roll page 40

Chocolate muffins page 164

Chocolate cookie torte page 142

Lemon poppy seed muffins page 156

Whole wheat carrot cake page 76

Madeleines page 146

Blueberry muffins page 162

Strawberry cheesecake page 194

French almond financiers
page 148

Black cherry cheesecake page 202

25

Tea party treats

Light fruitcake page 64

Lemon, lime, and poppy seed cake page 100

Tropical fruit and ginger cake page 72

Marble cake page 54

Apricot crumble shortbread page 134

Berry friands page 154

Banana, cranberry, and walnut loaf page 104

Marmalade and ginger loaf page 106

Orange and pistachio cake page 74

Lime drizzle cupcakes page 180

Sticky lemon cake page 68

Superfood loaf cake page 108

Victoria sponge cake page 38

After dinner

Mocha slice page 126

Toffee apple bake
page 138

White chocolate cakes
page 140

Rum and chocolate dacquoise
page 216

Apple streusel cake page 82

Pear and chocolate cake page 88

Honey cake page 58

Classic Pavlova page 214

Chocolate Amaretti roulade
page 50

Baked stem ginger cheesecake
page 200

Blueberry-ripple cheesecake
page 198

Mountain meringue cake
page 220

Black cherry cheesecake
page 202

**Rhubarb and ginger meringue
cake** page 218

SPONGE CAKES

Madeira cake

This traditional moist cake has a dense texture and a hint of lemon.

INGREDIENTS

3/4 cup plus 3 tbsp butter, at room temperature

3/4 cup sugar

3 eggs, lightly beaten

1 3/4 cups self-rising flour

juice of 1 lemon

METHOD

1 Preheat the oven to 350°F (180°C). Put the butter and sugar in a mixing bowl and beat with an electric mixer for 5 minutes or a wooden spoon, until pale and creamy.

2 Mixing all the time, add the eggs a little at a time, along with a little of the flour to stop the mixture from curdling. Stir in the lemon juice, then fold in the rest of the flour. Spoon the mixture into the lightly greased cake pan.

3 Bake for 1–1 1/2 hours, or until cooked through. To test, pierce the center of the cake with a skewer—if it comes out clean, the cake is cooked. Remove from the oven and leave to cool for 10 minutes in the pan, then run a knife around the edge to loosen. Leave to cool completely, then turn out onto a plate and serve.

serves 4–6

prep 15 mins
• cook
1–1 1/2 hrs

8in (20cm)
round cake pan

freeze for
up to 3 months

Vanilla sponge cake

This versatile sponge goes well with a number of fillings. This version uses buttercream and lemon curd for a zingy tartness to balance the vanilla.

INGREDIENTS

2 eggs, lightly beaten
$1/3$ cup sugar
a few drops of vanilla extract
$2/3$ cup self-rising flour
4 tbsp butter, at
    room temperature
1 cup (125g) confectioner's sugar
2 tbsp lemon curd

METHOD

1 Preheat the oven to 350°F (180°C). Put the eggs and sugar in a mixing bowl, and beat with a wire whisk or an electric mixer for 5 minutes, or until pale and creamy. Add a few drops of the vanilla extract.

2 Sift in the flour, a little at a time, folding each batch in gently before adding more. Pour the mixture into the lightly greased cake pan. Bake in the oven for 30 minutes, or until lightly golden. To test, pierce the center of the cake with a skewer—if it comes out clean, the cake is cooked. Remove from the oven, and leave to cool in the pan for 10–15 minutes, then loosen the edges with a knife and leave to cool completely.

3 Meanwhile, put the butter in a mixing bowl and beat with a wooden spoon for a few minutes until creamy. Sift in the confectioner's sugar, beat well, then add a few drops of vanilla extract and beat again. Remove the cake from the pan and slice in half horizontally. Cover the bottom half with the buttercream and the top half with the lemon curd. Sandwich together and serve.

serves 4–6

prep 15 mins
• cook 30 mins

8in (20cm)
round baking pan

freeze, before
filling, for up to
3 months

Angel food cake

Serve this light-as-air cake with your favorite summer berries.

INGREDIENTS

1 cup cake flour
$1/2$ cup confectioner's sugar
12 large egg whites
$1/2$ tsp cream of tartar
1 cup superfine sugar
1 tsp pure vanilla or almond extract

For the topping

$3/4$ cup heavy cream
3 tbsp confectioner's sugar
blueberries, raspberries, and strawberries, for serving

METHOD

1 Preheat the oven to 350°F (180°C). Sift the flour and confectioner's sugar together.

2 Beat the egg whites and cream of tartar in a large bowl with an electric mixer on high speed until soft peaks form. One tablespoon at a time, beat in the superfine sugar until shiny, stiff peaks form. In three additions, sift in the flour mixture, gently folding in each addition with a large rubber spatula. Fold in the vanilla. Spoon into a 10in (25cm) tube cake pan with a removable bottom and gently smooth the top.

3 Bake about 40 minutes, until the top is golden brown and springs back when pressed.

4 Invert the cake pan on a work surface. (The cake should clear the work surface—if not, perch the cake pan on ramekins.) Cool completely. Run a long, dull knife around the inside of the pan. Remove the sides of the pan. Pull the bottom of the cake away from tube section and transfer, upside down, to a serving platter.

5 To make the topping, whip the cream and confectioner's sugar until soft peaks form. Spoon over the cake. Cut into slices and serve with the berries. The cake is best served the day it is baked, and is good with any combination of fresh fruit.

serves 8–12

prep 30 mins,
plus cooling
• cook 40 mins

electric mixer
• 10in (25cm)
tube cake pan or
10in (25cm) angel
food cake pan

Victoria sponge cake

This light sponge cake is a perfect tea-party treat.

INGREDIENTS

³/₄ cup butter, at room temperature, plus more for the pans
1 cup granulated sugar
3 large eggs, at room temperature
1 cup plus 2 tbsp all-purpose flour
1 tsp baking powder
¹/₄ tsp salt
¹/₂ cup raspberry preserves
²/₃ cup heavy cream
confectioner's sugar, for topping

METHOD

1 Preheat the oven to 375°F (190°C). Lightly butter two 8in (20cm) round cake pans and line the bottoms with parchment paper.

2 Beat the butter and sugar together with an electric mixer on high speed for 3 minutes or with a wooden spoon for 5 minutes, or until very pale and fluffy. One at a time, beat in the eggs, beating well after each addition. Sift the flour, baking powder, and salt together. Add to the butter mixture and beat on low speed until smooth.

3 Divide the mixture equally between the cake pans and smooth the tops. Bake for 20–25 minutes, until the cakes spring back when pressed in the centers. Let cool on a wire rack for 5 minutes. Invert and unmold onto the rack, and peel off the parchment paper. Cool completely.

4 Place one cake layer upside down on a serving plate. Spread with the raspberry preserves. Lightly whip the cream until soft peaks form. Spread over the preserves. Top with the remaining layer, rounded side up. Sift confectioner's sugar over the top and serve immediately.

serves 8

prep 20 mins,
plus cooling
• cook 25 mins

for the best
results, have
all your
ingredients
at room
temperature

two 8in (20cm)
round baking
pans

freeze for
up to 1 month

Swiss roll

For best results, avoid overfilling the sponge to prevent spillage, and roll it while it is still slightly warm to avoid breaking.

INGREDIENTS

3 large eggs
$1/2$ cup granulated sugar, plus extra to sprinkle
1 tsp pure vanilla extract
$3/4$ cup self-rising flour
6 tbsp strawberry jam, raspberry jam,
    lemon curd, or Nutella

METHOD

1 Preheat the oven to 400°F (200°C). Line the bottom and sides of a 13 x 9 (32.5 x 23cm) jelly roll pan with parchment paper. In a large bowl set over a saucepan of simmering water, beat the eggs, sugar, and a pinch of salt with an electric mixer or a wire whisk for 5 minutes, or until very thick and creamy—any batter that drips from the beaters should rest on the surface for a few seconds before sinking in.

2 Remove the bowl from the saucepan and place it on a work surface. Beat the mixture for about 2 minutes, or until cool to the touch. Add the vanilla and sift in the flour, and fold in gently. Scrape into the prepared pan and gently spread in an even layer, reaching into the corners. Bake for 12–15 minutes or until the top is firm to the touch and the cake has shrunk from the sides of the pan.

3 Sprinkle a large sheet of parchment paper with granulated sugar, then invert the cake onto it. Let cool for 5 minutes, then carefully peel away the parchment that clings to the top of the cake. If the jam is too thick to spread, warm it in a saucepan, then spread it over the cake. Make a small indentation with the back of a knife along one of the short sides, about $3/4$in (2cm) in from the edge. With this side facing toward you, roll the cake into a cylinder, using the parchment paper to ease the process. When the cake is completely rolled up, leave to cool completely. Place the cake, seam-side down, on a serving plate. Dust with extra sugar before serving.

serves 8–10

prep 20 mins
• cook 15 mins

13 x 9in (32.5 x
23cm) jelly roll
pan

Chocolate and buttercream Swiss roll

This classic is always a hit at children's parties.

INGREDIENTS

3 large eggs
6 tbsp granulated sugar
$\frac{1}{2}$ cup all-purpose flour
$\frac{1}{4}$ cup unsweetened cocoa powder, plus extra for dusting
$\frac{1}{4}$ cup plus 1 tbsp butter, at room temperature
1 cup confectioner's sugar, sifted, plus extra for
   dusting (optional)

METHOD

1 Preheat the oven to 400°F (200°C). Place a large bowl over a pan of hot water, add the eggs and sugar, and beat with an electric mixer or wire whisk for 5–10 minutes, until the mixture is thick and creamy. Sift in the flour and cocoa powder and fold in with a spoon.

2 Line an 13 x 9in (20 x 30cm) jelly roll pan with parchment paper, then pour the mixture into the pan and level the top. Bake for 10 minutes, until the cake is springy to the touch. Remove from the oven, cover with a damp tea towel, and leave to cool slightly.

3 Turn the cake out onto a sheet of parchment paper dusted with cocoa powder. Put the butter in a mixing bowl and beat with an electric mixer or wooden spoon until creamy. Whisk in the confectioner's sugar a little at a time, then spread the mixture over the cake. Using the parchment paper to help you, roll the cake into a long cylinder, starting from one of the short sides. Dust with more cocoa powder if desired, and serve.

serves 8

prep 25 mins
• cook 10 mins

13 x 9in
(20 x 30cm)
jelly roll pan

Bienenstich

This German recipe is also known as Bee Sting Cake.

INGREDIENTS

1 cup all-purpose flour
1 tbsp butter, softened, plus more for the bowl
2 tsp sugar
1 tsp instant yeast
pinch of salt
1 large egg, beaten
crème pâtissière

For the glaze

2 tbsp butter
$4\frac{1}{4}$ tsp superfine sugar
1 tbsp honey
1 tbsp heavy cream
2 tbsp slivered almonds
1 tsp fresh lemon juicee

METHOD

1 Sift the flour into a bowl. Add the butter and rub it in with your fingertips until crumbly. Stir in the sugar, yeast, and salt. Add the egg and stir, adding enough water (about 3 tbsp) to make a soft dough.

2 Knead on a lightly floured surface for about 8 minutes, until smooth and elastic. Put in a buttered bowl, turn to coat, and cover with plastic wrap. Let stand in a warm place about 1 hour, or until doubled.

3 Preheat the oven to 375°F (190°C). Butter the cake pan and line with a round of parchment paper. Punch down the dough and roll into an 8in (20cm) circle. Transfer to the pan, cover with plastic wrap, and let stand for 20 minutes, until slightly puffy.

4 Meanwhile, to make the glaze, melt the butter in a saucepan over low heat. Add the sugar, honey, and cream and stir until the sugar dissolves. Increase the heat to medium and simmer for 3 minutes until reduced by about half. Stir in the almonds and lemon juice. Let cool.

5 Carefully spread the cooled glaze over the dough, cover with the wrap, and let rise for 10 minutes more. Bake for 20–25 minutes, tenting the cake with foil if it browns too quickly. Let cool in the pan for 30 minutes, then unmold and cool.

6 Slice the cake in half crosswise. Spread the crème pâtissière on the bottom half, place the almond layer on top, and transfer to a serving plate.

serves 8–10

prep 30 mins,
plus rising and
cooling
• cook 25 mins

8in (20cm)
round baking
pan

All-in-one chocolate cake with fudge frosting

This classic cake is a perennial favorite for birthdays and special treats.

INGREDIENTS

1³/₄ cups self-rising flour
¹/₄ cup unsweetened cocoa powder
1 tsp baking powder
4 large eggs
1 cup granulated sugar, plus 2 tbsp
1 cup butter, at room temperature
1 tsp pure vanilla extract

For the frosting

¹/₂ cup unsweetened cocoa powder
1¹/₄ cups confectioner's sugar
¹/₄ cup butter, melted
3 tbsp milk, plus a little extra if needed

METHOD

1 Preheat the oven to 350°F (180°C). Grease two 8in (20cm) round cake pans, then line with parchment paper. Sift the flour, cocoa, and baking powder into a large bowl. With an electric mixer or a wooden spoon, beat in the eggs, sugar, butter, and vanilla until well blended. Mix in 2 tablespoons of hot tap water. If the batter is too firm to easily drop off the beaters or spoon, add up to 2 more tablespoons of hot water. Divide the batter evenly between the pans and smooth the tops.

2 Bake for 35–40 minutes, or until risen and firm. Let cool in the pans for 5 minutes before unmolding onto racks to cool completely.

3 Meanwhile, to make the frosting, sift the cocoa powder and confectioner's sugar into a bowl, add the butter and milk, and beat until smooth. Add a little extra milk if the mixture is too thick to spread easily. Place one cooled cake layer on a serving plate and spread with half of the frosting. Align the second layer on top of the first, and spread with the remaining frosting, leaving the sides unfrosted.

SPONGE CAKES

serves 8–12

prep 20 mins
• cook 40 mins

two 8in (20cm)
round baking
pans

freeze, before
frosting, for up to
3 months

Chocolate roulade

Serve this festive dessert for the holidays as the French classic bûche de Noël.

INGREDIENTS

5 large eggs, at room temperature
$3/4$ cup granulated sugar
$3/4$ cup all-purpose flour
$1/3$ cup Dutch-process cocoa powder
$1/2$ tsp baking powder
confectioner's sugar, for dusting

For the filling and icing

$2/3$ cup heavy cream
5oz (150g) bittersweet chocolate, chopped
$1/2$ cup seedless raspberry preserves

METHOD

1 Preheat the oven to 350°F (180°C). Line a $15^1/_2$ x $10^1/_2$in (39 x 27cm) jelly roll pan with parchment paper.

2 Beat the eggs and sugar in a large bowl with an electric mixer at high speed, or a wire whisk, about 5 minutes, until the mixture has tripled in volume. Sift the flour, cocoa, and baking powder together. Sift over the egg mixture and carefully fold together.

3 Spread in the pan. Bake about 15 minutes, until the top springs back when pressed lightly with a finger. Sift confectioner's sugar over the cake. Place a clean kitchen towel and a cutting board over the jelly roll pan. Invert them together to unmold the cake. Remove the parchment paper and place on the cake. Roll up the cake, with the paper inside. Let cool.

4 Meanwhile, to make the icing, bring the cream to a boil in a small saucepan. Add the chocolate and stir until melted. Remove from the heat and let cool for 10 minutes.

5 Unroll the cake and discard the paper. Spread the preserves over the cake. Roll up the cake again. Place the roll on a wire rack, seam side down. Spread the icing all over the top, sides, and ends of the cake. Use a fork to create ridges down the length of the cake. Transfer to a platter. Just before serving, dust with confectioner's sugar.

serves 10

prep 30 mins
• cook 15 mins

15½ x 10½in
(39 x 27cm)
jelly roll pan

freeze for
up to 6 months

Chocolate Amaretti roulade

Crushed Amaretti cookies add crunch to this indulgent roulade.

INGREDIENTS

6 large eggs, separated
3/4 cup granulated sugar
1/2 cup unsweetened cocoa powder
confectioner's sugar, for dusting
1 cup heavy whipping cream
2–3 tbsp Amaretto or brandy
20 Amaretti cookies, crushed,
   plus 2 extra
13/4oz (50g) semisweet chocolate

METHOD

1 Preheat the oven to 350°F (180°C). Line a 13 x 9in (23 x 33cm) jelly roll pan with parchment paper. Combine the egg yolks and sugar in a large heatproof bowl set over a pan of simmering water, and beat with an electric mixer or wire whisk until pale, thick, and creamy, about 10 minutes. Remove from the heat. Put the egg whites in a mixing bowl and beat with an electric mixer or wire whisk until soft peaks form.

2 Sift the cocoa powder into the egg yolk mixture and gently fold in along with the egg whites. Scrape the batter into the pan. Bake for 20 minutes or until just firm to the touch. Loosen the edges with a knife and invert onto a sheet of parchment paper dusted with confectioner's sugar. Remove the pan, leaving the top parchment in place. Cool for 30 minutes.

3 Put the cream in a bowl and beat with an electric mixer or wire whisk until soft peaks form. Peel off the top parchment from the cake, and trim away any ragged edges. Drizzle the Amaretto or brandy over the surface of the cake, then spread with the cream, sprinkle with the crushed Amaretti cookies, and grate most of the chocolate over the top.

4 Starting from one of the short sides, roll the cake into a long cylinder, using the parchment to help keep it tightly together. Discard the parchment and place the roulade seam-side down on a plate. Crumble the extra cookies over the top, grate the remaining chocolate over them, and dust with confectioner's sugar.

serves 8

prep 30 mins
• cook 20 mins

13 x 9in
(23 x 33cm)
jelly roll pan

50

Sachertorte

This is Viennese baking at is finest—a rich chocolate cake glazed with a thin layer of apricot preserves and a finishing coat of shiny chocolate.

INGREDIENTS

1 cup plus 2 tbsp butter, at room temperature
1¼ cups sugar
9oz (250g) bittersweet chocolate, melted and tepid
½ tsp pure vanilla extract
5 large eggs, separated, at room temperature
1¾ cups all-purpose flour
½ cup apricot preserves

For the chocolate glaze

1¼ cups heavy cream
7oz (200g) dark chocolate, chopped
¼ tsp pure vanilla extract

METHOD

1 Preheat the oven to 350°F (180°C). Line a 9in (23cm) round cake pan with parchment paper.

2 Beat the butter and sugar together with an electric mixer until light and fluffy. Beat in the chocolate and vanilla. One at a time, beat in the egg yolks. Fold in the flour.

3 Beat the egg whites until stiff peaks form. Stir one-fourth of the whites into the batter, then fold in the remainder. Spread evenly in the pan.

4 Bake for 45–60 minutes, or until a wooden toothpick inserted in the center comes out clean. Transfer to a wire rack and let cool for 10 minutes. Invert and unmold the cake. Remove the parchment paper. Let cool completely.

5 To make the glaze, bring the cream to a simmer in a small saucepan over medium heat. Remove from the heat and add the chocolate and vanilla. Let stand until the chocolate softens, then stir until smooth. Let cool, stirring occasionally, until it thickens slightly.

6 Melt the apricot preserves in a small saucepan over low heat. Strain through a sieve. Slice the cake in half horizontally. Spread the lower layer with some of the apricot mixture. Return the top layer. Spread the remaining apricot mixture over the top of the cake, then use a metal spatula to smooth it evenly over the top and sides. Let cool until set.

7 Place the cake on a wire rack over a baking sheet. Transfer ¼ cup of the glaze to a small bowl. Pour the remaining chocolate glaze over the cake. Use a metal spatula to smooth the glaze over the top and sides of the cake. Patch any unglazed spots with the glaze that runs onto the baking sheet. Refrigerate about 10 minutes, until the glaze sets.

8 If necessary, warm the reserved glaze until fluid. Transfer to a small plastic food storage bag and force into a corner of the bag. Snip off the corner of the bag with kitchen scissors. Squeeze the glaze out of the bag to write "Sacher" over the top of the cake in flowing script. Let cool, and serve with whipped cream.

serves 8–12

prep 40 mins, plus cooling
• cook 60 mins

9in (23cm) round baking pan
• electric mixer

freeze, undecorated, for up to 3 months

Marble cake

The marbled effect is a clever swirl of plain and chocolate batters.

INGREDIENTS

$1^1/_2$ cups butter, softened
$1^3/_4$ cups granulated sugar
6 large eggs, at room temperature
1 tsp pure vanilla extract
$2^2/_3$ cups all-purpose flour
4 tsp baking powder
$^1/_2$ tsp salt
$^1/_2$ cup milk
3 tbsp natural or Dutch process cocoa powder
confectioner's sugar, for dusting

METHOD

1 Preheat the oven to 350°F (180°C). Butter and flour the pan, tapping out the excess flour.

2 Beat the butter and sugar until fluffy, with an electric mixer on high speed or a wooden spoon, about 3 minutes. One at a time, beat in the eggs, beating well after each, then beat in the vanilla.

3 Sift together the flour, baking powder, and salt. On low speed, beat in half the flour mix. Beat in the milk, then the remaining flour mix.

4 Spoon one-third of the batter into the pan. Transfer half the remaining batter into another bowl. Sift in the cocoa powder and stir. Spoon dollops of the cocoa batter into the pan, then top with the plain batter. Swirl a knife through the two batters to create a pattern, taking care not to over-mix. Bake for about 45 minutes.

5 Cool in the pan for 10 minutes, then remove. Dust with confectioner's sugar and serve.

serves 12

prep 30 mins
• cook 45 mins

9in (23cm)
kugelhopf
mold or
14 x 4½in
(35 × 11cm)
baking pan

SPONGE CAKES

Pecan, coffee, and maple cake

This rich, sweet cake is perfect with coffee.

INGREDIENTS

2 cups self-rising flour
1 cup granulated sugar
$^3/_4$ cup butter, at room temperature
3 large eggs, lightly beaten
$^1/_2$ cup sour cream
2 tbsp brewed espresso or strong coffee, or more as needed
$^1/_2$ cup chopped pecans

For the icing

$3^1/_2$ tbsp butter
1 tbsp pure maple syrup
2 cups confectioner's sugar
2 tbsp brewed espresso or strong coffee
about 20 pecan halves or $^1/_3$ cup chopped pecans, for garnish

METHOD

1 Preheat the oven to 350°F (180°C). Lightly grease two 8in (18cm) round cake pans and line the bottoms with parchment paper. In a large bowl, beat the sugar and butter with an electric mixer or wooden spoon until light and fluffy, about 2 minutes. Beat in the eggs one at time, beating well after each addition, then beat in the sour cream and espresso. Sift the flour into the bowl and add the pecans; fold until the flour is just incorporated and the pecans are mixed throughout. Divide the batter evenly between the pans and level the tops.

2 Bake for 35–40 minutes until risen, firm to the touch, and slightly shrunken from the sides of the pans. Let cool for 5 minutes in the pans, then unmold onto a wire rack to cool completely.

3 Meanwhile, make the icing. Melt the butter with the maple syrup in a small pan. Sift the sugar into a bowl, add the butter and syrup mixture along with the coffee and beat with an electric mixer or wooden spoon until thick and smooth. Spread the icing over the tops of the two cooled cakes, then sandwich together. Decorate the top of the cake with pecans.

serves 8

prep 15 mins
• cook 40 mins

two 8in
(20cm) round
baking pans

freeze, before
icing, for up to
2 months

Honey cake

The unusual pairing of prunes and sweetened sour cream makes this a novel —and delicious—variation on a Russian honey cake.

INGREDIENTS

$^1/_2$ cup unsalted butter

5 tbsp honey

2 large eggs

3 cups all-purpose flour

$^1/_2$ tsp baking powder

1 Earl Grey teabag

3 cups pitted prunes

1 cup light brown sugar (packed)

$1^1/_4$ cups sour cream

METHOD

1 Place the butter and honey in a bowl and cream together thoroughly. Beat in the eggs, then fold in the flour and baking powder with a metal spoon. Mix together to form a dough. Wrap the dough in plastic wrap and refrigerate for 2 hours.

2 Remove the dough from the refrigerator and leave to come to room temperature—about 30 minutes.

3 Make the tea by pouring $^1/_2$ cup boiling water over the teabag in a heatproof bowl. Leave for 3 minutes, then strain the tea into a small saucepan. Add the prunes and half the sugar. Bring to a boil, then remove from the heat and leave to cool.

4 Preheat the oven to 350°F (180°C). Line a large baking sheet with parchment paper. Divide the dough into 6 equal balls, then roll out each ball on a lightly floured surface to a thickness of about $^1/_8$in (3mm). Cut the dough into large circles, using a 6in (15cm) diameter bowl or plate to cut around.

5 Place 2 rounds onto the prepared baking sheet and bake for 5–10 minutes, or until golden. Remove from the oven and transfer to a wire rack to cool. Allow baking sheet to cool, then repeat with the remaining rounds.

6 Stir the sour cream in a bowl with the remaining half of the sugar until the mixture is smooth. Place the rounds separately on a plate or clean work surface and spread each generously with the sweetened sour cream.

7 Assemble the cake on a serving plate. Start with a cream-topped round, spoon a layer of prunes and tea syrup over it, and top with another cream-topped round. Repeat until all the cream-topped rounds have been used. Finish with a generous drizzle of tea syrup and prunes on the top. Cover carefully and refrigerate for 2 hours before serving.

PREPARE AHEAD The cake can be stored for up to 2 days in the refrigerator.

serves 6

prep 20 mins, plus chilling, resting, and assembling
• cook 30 mins

allow 2 hrs for chilling, and 2 hrs for sitting

large baking sheet
• 6in (15cm) round bowl or plate

freeze the uncooked dough for up to 3 months

Chocolate almond cake

This dense, moist cake is made even richer with a ganache topping.

INGREDIENTS

5oz (140g) bittersweet chocolate, chopped
$1/2$ cup plus 2 tbsp butter, at room temperature, plus more for the pan
$3/4$ cup sugar
3 large eggs, separated
$1/2$ cup almond flour (almond meal)
$1/2$ cup fresh bread crumbs
$1/2$ tsp baking powder
1 tbsp brandy or rum
$1/4$ tsp almond extract

For the ganache

5oz (140g) bittersweet chocolate, chopped
$1/4$ cup plus 2 tbsp butter

METHOD

1 Preheat the oven to 350°F (180°C). Butter an 8in (20cm) springform pan. Line with parchment paper and dust with flour.

2 Melt the chocolate in a heatproof bowl over a saucepan of simmering water. Remove from the heat and cool until tepid.

3 Beat the butter and sugar in a bowl with an electric mixer for 3 minutes, until pale and creamy. One at a time, beat in the egg yolks, then the chocolate. Stir in the almonds, bread crumbs, baking powder, brandy, and almond extract.

4 Beat the egg whites in another bowl until they form soft peaks. Fold into the batter. Spread in the pan.

5 Bake for 25 minutes, or until a wooden toothpick inserted in the center comes out clean. Let cool for 15 minutes on a wire rack. Invert and release the cake onto the rack set over a baking sheet. Remove the paper. Let cool completely.

6 To make the ganache, melt the butter in a heatproof bowl set over a saucepan of simmering water. Add the chocolate and stir until melted. Pour the ganache over the cake and spread over the top and sides with a metal spatula. Let the ganache set. Cut into slices and serve.

serves 6–8

prep 30 mins
• cook 25 mins

8in (20cm)
round
springform
pan
• electric mixer

freeze for
up to 1 month

Light fruitcake

In contrast to traditional heavy fruitcakes, this recipe is a good everyday bake.

INGREDIENTS

$^3/_4$ tbsp butter, at room temperature

1 cup light brown sugar (packed)

3 large eggs

$2^1/_4$ cups self-rising flour, sifted

2–3 tbsp whole milk

3 cups mixed dried fruit, coarsely chopped if needed

METHOD

1 Preheat the oven to 350°F (180°C). Line the bottom and sides of a 9in (23cm) round cake pan with parchment paper. In a bowl, beat the butter and sugar together with an electric mixer or wooden spoon until pale and creamy, then beat in the eggs, one at a time, adding 1 tablespoon of the flour after each one. Stir in the rest of the flour and the milk until well-blended—the mixture should drop easily off the beaters or spoon. Stir in the dried fruit.

2 Scrape the batter into the prepared pan, level the top, and bake for 1 hour 25 minutes–1 hour 40 minutes, or until firm to the touch and a skewer inserted into the middle of the cake comes out clean. Leave in the pan to cool completely on a wire rack.

serves 8–12

prep 25 mins
• cook 1 hr
40 mins

9in (23cm)
round baking
pan

freeze for
up to 3 months

Apricot cake

This light-as-a-feather cake has a winning combination of apricot and cinnamon flavors and a crunchy sugary topping.

INGREDIENTS

$^1/_2$ cup dried apricots, chopped
    into $^1/_2$in pieces
6 large eggs, separated
$^1/_2$ cup superfine sugar,
    plus 1 tbsp to sprinkle
juice of 1 lemon
$1^1/_4$ cups all-purpose flour, sifted
2 tbsp unsalted butter
$^1/_2$ tsp ground cinnamon

METHOD

1 Preheat the oven to 350°F (180°C). Grease a 9in springform pan and line with parchment paper. Place the chopped apricots in a bowl with enough cold water to cover, and leave to soak for 20 minutes. Drain and set aside.

2 Place the egg yolks and sugar in a large bowl, and beat with a handheld electric mixer for about 5 minutes until thick, creamy, and pale, and tripled in volume. Add the lemon juice and beat to combine. Fold in the flour thoroughly with a metal spoon, then set aside.

3 Place the egg whites in a large, clean, dry glass or metal bowl and beat, using an electric mixer with clean beaters, until the whites form soft peaks. Fold half the beaten egg white into the cake batter with a metal spoon, then fold in the remaining half.

4 Transfer $^1/_3$ of the batter to the prepared pan, spread it to level, then layer $^1/_3$ of the apricots on top. Add another $^1/_3$ of the cake mix, and top with another $^1/_3$ of the apricots. Spread the final $^1/_3$ of the cake mix on top, followed by the remaining apricots.

5 Melt the butter in a small saucepan over low heat, then drizzle over the apricots. Mix the cinnamon with the remaining 1 tbsp of sugar in a small bowl, and sprinkle evenly over the top.

6 Bake in the center of the oven for 40–45 minutes, or until the top is golden and springy, and a skewer inserted into the center of the cake comes out clean. Remove from the oven and leave to cool completely in the pan—the cake will shrink from the sides of the pan—then release the springform.

GOOD WITH Berries and cream as a dessert.

serves 6

prep 15 mins,
plus soaking
• cook 45 mins

eat on the day
of making

9in (23cm)
round
springform
pan
• handheld
electric mixer

Sticky lemon cake

The combination of fresh lemon juice and yogurt gives this cake a wonderfully fresh taste and moist texture.

INGREDIENTS

2 lemons
$^3/_4$ cup unsalted butter
$1^1/_4$ cups sugar
2 large eggs, plus one egg yolk
$1^1/_3$ cups almond flour (almond meal)
$^1/_2$ cup all-purpose flour
2 tsp baking powder
$1^1/_3$ cups plain yogurt

METHOD

1 Preheat the oven to 325°F (170°C). Butter an 8in (20cm) cake pan, and line the bottom with a round of parchment paper.

2 Grate the zest and squeeze the juice from the lemons; you should have 6 tbsp juice. Cream together the butter and $^3/_4$ cup sugar, and the zest in a large bowl until light and fluffy. Beat in the eggs, one at a time.

3 Whisk the flours and the baking powder together to eliminate any lumps. Stir into the butter mixture, followed by the yogurt and 2 tbsp of the lemon juice.

4 Spread in the pan. Bake for 30 minutes, or until the center springs back when pressed.

5 Meanwhile, stir the remaining $^1/_2$ cup sugar and 4 tbsp lemon juice in a saucepan over low heat to dissolve the sugar. Cool.

6 Transfer the cake to a wire rack. Pierce the cake all over with a skewer and drizzle the syrup on top. Cool for 30 minutes. Invert onto the rack, remove the pan, peel off the paper, and cool completely.

serves 8

prep 15 mins
• cook 30 mins

8in (20cm)
round baking
pan

Cherry and almond cake

Fresh, juicy cherries make this sponge a delicious contrast to dried-fruit cakes.

INGREDIENTS

$^1/_2$ cup plus 3 tbsp butter, at room temperature

$^3/_4$ cup granulated sugar

2 large eggs, lightly beaten

$2^1/_4$ cups self-rising flour, sifted

1 tsp baking powder

2 cups ground almonds

1 tsp pure vanilla extract

about $^2/_3$ cup whole milk

1lb (450g) cherries, stemmed and pitted

$^1/_4$ cup slivered almonds, chopped

confectioner's sugar, for dusting (optional)

METHOD

1 Preheat the oven to 350°F (180°C). Lightly grease an 8in (20cm) round springform pan and line the bottom with parchment paper. In a bowl, beat together the butter and sugar with an electric mixer until pale and creamy. Beat in the eggs one at a time, adding 1 tablespoon of the flour before adding the second egg.

2 Mix in the remaining flour, baking powder, ground almonds, and vanilla. Stir in $^1/_3$ cup of the milk. The batter should drop easily from the beaters. If the batter is too thick, gradually stir in the remaining milk. Mix in half of the cherries, then scrape the batter into the pan. Scatter with the remaining cherries, and then the almonds.

3 Bake for 1 hour 30 minutes–1 hour 45 minutes or until golden and firm to the touch. The exact cooking time will depend upon how juicy the cherries are. To test, insert a skewer into the cake—if there is uncooked batter on it, bake 5 minutes longer. If the surface of the cake starts to brown too much before it is fully baked, cover with foil. Transfer the pan to a wire rack to cool completely. Just before serving, release the sides of the springform and dust with confectioner's sugar.

serves 8–10

prep 20 mins,
plus cooling
• cook 1 hr 45 mins

8in (20cm)
springform
cake pan
• electric mixer
• wooden
skewer

Tropical fruit and ginger cake

This delicious sticky cake offers a new twist on traditional gingerbread-type cakes.

INGREDIENTS

$^1/_3$ cup light corn syrup

$^1/_3$ cup molasses

$^1/_3$ cup dried mango, thinly sliced

$^1/_3$ cup dried pineapple, thinly sliced

$^1/_3$ cup pitted dates, coarsely chopped

$^1/_2$ cup unsalted butter, softened

$^1/_2$ cup light brown sugar (packed)

2 large eggs, beaten

$2^1/_2$ cups all-purpose flour

$1^1/_2$ tsp baking soda

1 tsp salt

1 tsp ground cinnamon

1 tsp ground ginger

For the syrup

grated zest and juice of 1 lemon

$^1/_4$ cup light brown sugar (packed)

METHOD

1 Place the light corn syrup, molasses, and 1 cup water in a large saucepan and bring to a boil. Add the mango, pineapple, and dates, and simmer gently for 5 minutes. Pour the fruit and liquid on to a tray or shallow plate, and leave to cool at room temperature for about 15 minutes.

2 Preheat the oven to 350°F (180°C). Grease the pan and line with parchment paper.

3 Place the butter and sugar in a large bowl and cream with a handheld electric mixer until light and fluffy. Beat in the eggs gradually. Sift the flour, baking soda, salt, cinnamon, and ginger over the top, then add the cooled fruit mix. Fold in gently.

4 Transfer the mixture to the prepared pan and bake in the center of the oven for 50 minutes, or until the cake feels firm in the center. Remove from the oven and leave in the pan while you make the syrup.

5 To make the syrup, place the lemon zest and juice, $^1/_4$ cup water, and the sugar in a small saucepan. Heat gently to melt the sugar, then boil for 3–4 minutes to reduce to a slightly sticky syrup.

6 Prick the top of the cake all over with a skewer, then pour the hot syrup over the surface, letting it soak into the holes. Leave to cool completely in the pan before releasing the springform.

PREPARE AHEAD The cake can be stored for up to 5 days in an airtight container.

serves 8

prep 20 mins
• cook 1 hr

9in (23 cm)
springform pan
• handheld
electric mixer

freeze for
up to 3 months

Orange and pistachio cake

Yogurt gives this zesty, nutty cake a dense, moist texture.

INGREDIENTS

$^3/_4$ cup butter, at room temperature
1 cup granulated sugar
2 large eggs
$1^1/_2$ cups self-rising flour
$^3/_4$ cup Greek-style plain yogurt
$^1/_2$ cup pistachio nuts, finely chopped
$^1/_2$ cup blanched almonds, finely chopped
finely grated zest and juice of 1 orange
finely grated zest and juice of 1 lemon
1 tsp baking powder
mascarpone, to serve (optional)

METHOD

1 Preheat the oven to 350°F (180°C). Put the butter and sugar in a large bowl and beat with an electric mixer for 5 minutes or until pale and creamy. Beat in the eggs one at a time, along with a few tablespoons of the flour to prevent the mixture from curdling.

2 Beat in the yogurt, pistachio nuts, almonds, orange zest and juice, and lemon zest and juice. Mix well to form a smooth batter. Sift in the remaining flour and the baking powder, and carefully fold into the mixture. Pour into a lightly greased 8in (20cm) round springform pan.

3 Bake for 50–55 minutes, or until a skewer inserted into the center of the cake comes out clean. Remove from the oven and leave to cool in the pan for 10 minutes, then release the sides of the springform and leave on a wire rack to cool completely. Slice and serve with a dollop of mascarpone, if desired.

serves 6

prep 15 mins
• cook 55 mins

electric mixer
• 8in (20cm)
round
springform pan

freeze for
up to 3 months

Whole wheat carrot cake

This delicious, fiber-rich cake has a healthful profile.

INGREDIENTS

2 cups whole wheat pastry flour
2 tsp baking powder
2 tsp ground allspice
1 tsp ground ginger
$\frac{1}{2}$ tsp salt
1 cup light brown sugar (packed)
1 cup butter, at room temperature
6 large eggs, beaten
grated zest of 2 oranges
1 tsp pure vanilla extract
6 small carrots, peeled and coarsely grated (2 cups)
1 cup raisins or golden raisins
8oz (225g) cream cheese
1 cup confectioner's sugar
$\frac{1}{4}$ cup fresh orange juice

METHOD

1 Preheat the oven to 350°F (180°C). Butter two 8in (20cm) round cake pans, and line the bottoms with parchment paper. Whisk the flour, baking powder, allspice, ginger, and salt in a large bowl, then stir in the sugar. Add the butter, eggs, vanilla, and half the zest. Beat with a wooden spoon or an electric mixer set on high speed about 2 minutes, or until the mixture is smooth. Stir in the carrots and raisins.

2 Spread the batter in the pans. Bake for about 25 minutes or until a toothpick inserted in the center comes out clean. Transfer to a wire rack and cool for 10 minutes. Invert, peel off the paper, turn right-side up, and cool completely.

3 Meanwhile, make the frosting. Beat the cream cheese, remaining orange zest, and confectioner's sugar. Add enough orange juice to make a spreadable frosting. Spread $\frac{1}{2}$ cup of the frosting over 1 cake layer, top with the other layer, and frost with the remainder.

serves 8

prep 15 mins
• cook 25 mins

2 x 8in (20cm)
round cake pans

Almond and orange cake

This cake does not need flour or butter, so it's great for people on restricted diets.

INGREDIENTS

7oz (200g) carrots, peeled and sliced
1 tbsp fresh orange juice, or orange- or almond-flavored liqueur
4 large eggs, separated
$1/2$ tsp pure vanilla extract
grated zest of 1 orange
$3/4$ cup sugar
$1^1/4$ cup almond flour (almond meal)
confectioner's sugar, for sifting (optional)

METHOD

1 Preheat the oven to 325°F (170°C). Butter an 8in (20cm) round cake pan and line the bottom with a round of parchment paper.

2 Cook the carrots in a little water for about 15 minutes, or until very tender. Drain and purée with the orange juice; you should have $1/2$ cup of purée.

3 Beat the egg yolks, vanilla, and orange zest in a large bowl with an electric mixer on high speed. Gradually add the sugar, mixing until batter becomes very thick. Stir in the carrot purée and almond flour.

4 In a clean, dry bowl, with clean beaters, beat the egg whites until stiff, then fold into the batter. Spread in the pan. Bake for 30 minutes or until a toothpick inserted into the center comes out clean.

5 Transfer to a wire rack and cool for 10 minutes. Invert onto the rack, peel off the paper, and cool completely. Sift confectioner's sugar over the top before serving, if desired.

GOOD WITH Fresh fruit, such as raspberries, blackberries, or blueberries, and a spoonful of Greek yogurt or whipped cream.

serves 8

prep 10 mins
• cook 45 mins

8in (20cm)
round
baking pan
• food
processor
• electric mixer

Coconut and lime cake

Layers of tangy lime and coconut sponge with cream cheese frosting make this cake an attractive centerpiece your guests will love.

INGREDIENTS

2 cups self-rising flour
1 cup plus 2 tbsp granulated sugar
1 cup butter, at room temperature
4 large eggs, lightly beaten
$^2/_3$ cup shredded coconut
finely grated zest of 1 lime
2 tbsp fresh lime juice

For the frosting

1 cup confectioner's sugar, or more as needed
finely grated zest of 1 lime
2 tbsp fresh lime juice
10oz (300g) cream cheese, at room temperature
2 tbsp toasted shredded coconut

METHOD

1 Preheat the oven to 350°F (180°C). Grease an 8in (20cm) round cake pan or springform pan that is at least 3in (7cm) deep. Line the bottom with parchment paper. Sift the flour into a large bowl, add the sugar, butter, and eggs, and beat with an electric mixer or wooden spoon until well blended. Stir in the coconut, lime zest, and lime juice. Scrape into the prepared pan and level the top. Bake for 1 hour–1 hour 15 minutes or until risen and firm to the touch. Let cool for 5 minutes in the pan, then unmold onto a wire rack to cool completely. Using a serrated knife, carefully slice the cake horizontally into three equal layers.

2 To make the frosting, sift the confectioner's sugar into a bowl, add the lime zest, lime juice, and cream cheese, and beat with an electric mixer or wooden spoon until well blended. Taste, adding more sugar if needed. Spread the frosting over the three layers of the cake, then sandwich them together. Scatter the toasted coconut over the top.

serves 8

prep 20 mins, plus cooling
• cook 1 hr 15 mins

8in (20cm) round baking pan or springform

freeze, before frosting, for up to 3 months

Apple streusel cake

German in origin, streusel is a sweet, sometimes spiced, crumb mixture.

INGREDIENTS

1¼ cups all-purpose flour
½ cup plus 1 tbsp butter, at room temperature
⅔ cup granulated sugar
1 tsp ground cinnamon
2 large eggs, lightly beaten
½ tsp vanilla extract
1 Granny Smith apple, peeled, cored, and cut into chunks
½ cup golden raisins

For the streusel topping

1 cup all-purpose flour
½ cup granulated sugar or light brown sugar (packed)
⅓ cup ground almonds
1 tsp ground cinnamon
5 tbsp butter, cubed

METHOD

1 Preheat the oven to 350°F (180°C). Lightly grease an 8in (20cm) round springform pan, and line the bottom with parchment paper. Sift the flour into a bowl, add the butter, sugar, cinnamon, eggs, and vanilla, and beat with an electric mixer until light and creamy. Scrape the batter into the pan, and scatter the apple and raisins on the top.

2 To make the topping: In another bowl, stir together the flour, sugar, ground almonds, and cinnamon. Rub the cubed butter into the mixture with your fingertips until it resembles coarse bread crumbs. Scatter an even layer of the topping over the fruit, pressing down gently. Bake for 1 hour 20 minutes or until a skewer inserted into the cake comes out clean or with only a bit of moist fruit clinging to it. Let cool in the pan for at least 20 minutes before releasing the sides of the springform.

GOOD WITH Custard, ice cream, or cream.

serves 8

prep 20 mins
• cook 1 hr
20 mins

8in (20cm)
round
springform
cake pan
• electric
mixer

Tropical angel cake

Exotic fruits are a perfect partner to this coconut-flavored angel food cake.

INGREDIENTS

4 large egg whites
$1/2$ tsp cream of tartar
$3/4$ cup granulated sugar
$1/2$ cup all-purpose flour
4 tsp cornstarch
$1/3$ cup shredded coconut

For the topping

8oz (200g) Greek-style plain yogurt
1 cup mixed peeled and chopped tropical fruit, such as pineapple
   and mango
seeds and pulp from 2 passion fruits
finely grated lime zest, for garnish

METHOD

1 Preheat the oven to 375°F (190°C). Put the egg whites, cream of tartar, and 1 tbsp cold water in a mixing bowl and beat with an electric mixer until the mixture forms stiff peaks. Beat in the sugar 1 tbsp at a time until the mixture is stiff and shiny.

2 Sift the flour and cornstarch into the mixture, then fold in the coconut. Carefully spoon the batter into an ungreased 9in (23cm) savarin ring mold and smooth the top, pressing down gently to remove any air spaces. Bake for 15 minutes, then reduce the oven temperature to 350°F (180°C) and bake for another 15 minutes, until the top of the cake is firm to the touch and golden brown.

3 Place the pan on a wire rack and let cool completely. Carefully ease the cake out of the pan with a blunt knife and unmold onto a serving plate.

4 To make the topping, lightly beat the yogurt until smooth and creamy, then spoon into the center of the cake. Top with the fruit, and drizzle with the passion fruit seeds. Scatter the lime zest over the top.

serves 6–8

**prep 15 mins
• cook 30 mins**

**electric mixer
• 9in (23cm)
savarin
ring mold**

Apple fruitcake

In Britain, this dense fruitcake is a popular choice for celebrations. This may just be the best fruitcake you ever had.

INGREDIENTS

2$\frac{1}{2}$ cups raisins

2 cups pitted chopped prunes

2 cups candied cherries

2 cups peeled, cored, and finely chopped
    Golden Delicious apples

1$\frac{1}{3}$ cups golden raisins

2$\frac{1}{2}$ cups hard apple or pear cider

4 tsp pumpkin pie spice blend

2 cups all-purpose flour

2 tsp baking powder

$\frac{1}{2}$ teaspoon salt

$\frac{3}{4}$ cup butter, at room temperature

$\frac{3}{4}$ cup dark brown sugar (packed)

3 large eggs, beaten

1$\frac{1}{4}$ cups almond flour (almond meal)

For the decoration

8oz (225g) ready-to-roll fondant

confectioner's sugar, for rolling

3 tbsp apricot preserves, warmed and strained

METHOD

1 The day before baking, bring all the fruit, cider, and spice to a simmer. Cover and simmer for 20 minutes, or until most of the liquid has been absorbed. Remove from the heat, cover, and let stand at least 12 hours at room temperature.

2 Preheat the oven to 325°F (170°C) Lightly butter the cake pan and line the bottom and sides with parchment paper.

3 Sift the flour, baking powder, and salt together. Cream the butter and sugar with a wooden spoon or an electric mixer, about 3 minutes. Gradually beat in the eggs. Stir in the flour mixture and ground almonds, then the soaked fruit and its liquid. Spread the batter evenly in the pan.

4 Bake for about 2$\frac{1}{2}$ hours, or until a wooden skewer inserted into the center of the cake comes out clean. Transfer to a rack and cool for 15 minutes. Invert and unmold the cake, remove the paper, and let cool.

5 Knead the fondant and roll into a 9in (23cm) square about $\frac{1}{8}$in (3mm) thick. Brush the cake with the preserves. Place the fondant on the cake. Cut into pieces and serve.

PREPARE AHEAD The day before, cook the fruit in the cider. Leave to cool and store in a cool place.

serves 16

prep 25 mins,
plus soaking
• cook 2 hrs
30 mins

complete step
1 a day ahead,
then allow fruit
to soak
overnight

8–10in
(20–25cm)
deep square
baking pan

Pear and chocolate cake

This luscious cake is an excellent choice when you want to impress.

INGREDIENTS

$^1/_2$ cup butter, softened
$^3/_4$ cup light brown sugar (packed)
4 large eggs, lightly beaten
$2^1/_4$ cups self-rising flour, sifted
$^1/_2$ cup unsweetened cocoa powder
$^1/_2$ cup chopped dark or semisweet chocolate
2 ripe pears, peeled, cored, and chopped
$^2/_3$ cup whole milk
confectioner's sugar, to dust

METHOD

1 Preheat the oven to 350°F (180°C). Line the bottom of an 8in (20cm) springform pan with parchment paper, and grease the sides with butter.

2 Beat the butter with the sugar until pale and creamy. Beat the eggs in gradually, adding a little of the flour each time. Fold in the cocoa powder, chopped chocolate, and pears. Mix in the milk, just until blended.

3 Pour the batter into the prepared cake pan, place it in the oven, and bake for about 30 minutes, or until firm and springy to the touch. Allow to cool in the pan for 5 minutes, then remove the tin, and transfer the cake to a wire rack to cool completely. Dust with confectioner's sugar before serving.

GOOD WITH A scoop of rich vanilla ice cream.

serves 6–8

prep 30 mins
• cook 30 mins

8in (20cm)
round
springform
pan

Toffee-topped banana cake

This big cake is ideal for large family gatherings or other occasions where you need to feed a crowd.

INGREDIENTS

$^3/_4$ cup unsalted butter, softened
$^3/_4$ cup light brown sugar (packed)
4 eggs, beaten
$1^1/_4$ cup Brazil nuts, chopped
3 large ripe bananas, peeled and mashed
$^1/_4$ tsp apple pie spice blend or ground cinnamon
3 cups self-rising flour
1 tsp baking powder
$1^1/_4$ cups Greek-style plain yogurt mixed with 1 tbsp honey

For the topping

$^1/_3$ cup unsalted butter
$^3/_4$ cup light brown sugar (packed)
2 tbsp heavy cream
$^3/_4$ cup Brazil nuts, chopped

METHOD

1 Preheat the oven to 350°F (180°C). Grease the cake pan and line with parchment paper.

2 Place the butter and sugar in a large bowl and cream together until light and fluffy. Beat in the eggs, a little at a time. Stir in the Brazil nuts, bananas, and spice. Sift the flour and baking powder over the mix, add the yogurt and honey and fold in gently with a metal spoon.

3 Transfer to the prepared cake pan, making sure the mix is evenly distributed, especially to the edges of the pan. Bake for about 1 hour 20 minutes, or until a skewer inserted into the center of the cake comes out clean. Carefully place the oven rack 6–8 inches (15–20cm) from the broiler, then preheat the broiler.

4 For the topping, place the butter, sugar, and cream in a saucepan. Bring to a simmer point, stirring until the sugar is dissolved. Remove from the heat and stir in the Brazil nuts.

5 Spread the toffee mix evenly over the cake, then place the cake under the preheated broiler for 1–2 minutes, being careful to avoid burning. Leave to cool completely in the pan. Use a blunt knife to loosen the cake and topping, then release the springform.

PREPARE AHEAD The cake can be stored in an airtight container for up to 2 days.

serves 10–12

**prep 15 mins
• cook 1 hr
22 mins**

**8in (20cm)
round
springform pan**

Black Forest gâteau

The German Black Forest region is not just the home of the cuckoo clock, but the namesake of one of the most popular of all chocolate cakes.

INGREDIENTS

6 large eggs
1 cup sugar
1 cup all-purpose flour
$1/2$ cup cocoa powder
6 tbsp melted butter
1 tsp pure vanilla extract

2 x 15oz (420g) cans pitted black cherries
$1/4$ cup Kirsch
$2^{1}/4$ cups heavy cream
5oz (140g) bittersweet chocolate, grated
   on a box grater

METHOD

1 Preheat the oven to 350°F (180°C). Lightly butter a 9in (23cm) springform pan and line the bottom with parchment paper. Combine the eggs and sugar in a large heatproof bowl. Place over a saucepan of simmering water. Whisk just until the mixture is hot and the sugar is melted. Beat with a wire whisk or an electric mixer on high speed, about 5 minutes, or until pale and tripled in volume.

2 Sift the flour and cocoa together. In two additions, sift over the egg mixture and fold in. Mix together the melted butter and vanilla. Stir about 1 cup of the batter into the butter mixture, then fold back into the batter. Spread in the pan. Bake about 40 minutes, or until the top springs back when pressed in the center. Let cool 5 minutes on a wire rack. Remove the sides of the pan, invert, and remove the bottom of the pan and parchment paper. Let cool.

3 Using a long serrated knife, carefully cut the cake into three layers. Drain one can of cherries and mix 6 tbsp of the juice with the Kirsch. Roughly chop the drained cherries. Whip the cream until soft peaks form.

4 Place one cake layer onto a serving platter. Drizzle with one third of the Kirsch syrup. Spread with a thin layer of whipped cream and half the chopped cherries. Repeat with another cake layer. Top with the final layer and remaining syrup. Using a metal spatula, spread the whipped cream over the top and sides of the cake. Transfer the remaining cream to a pastry bag fitted with a star-shaped tip.

5 Using a large spoon, press the grated chocolate on the sides of the cake. Pipe swirls of cream around the top edge of the cake. Drain the second can of cherries and fill the center of the cake with the cherries. Serve chilled.

PREPARE AHEAD The cake can be made up to 3 days in advance. Store in the refrigerator until ready to serve.

serves 8

prep 55 mins
• cook 40 mins

9in (23cm)
springform pan
• piping bag and
star-shaped
frosting tip

freeze for
up to 1 month

LOAF CAKES

Banana bread

This moist cake keeps beautifully.

INGREDIENTS

1³/₄ cups all-purpose flour
1¹/₂ tsp baking powder
6 tbsp butter, plus more for the pan
²/₃ cup packed light brown sugar
3 ripe bananas
¹/₂ cup plain low-fat yogurt
2 large eggs
³/₄ cup walnuts, chopped

METHOD

1 Preheat the oven to 350°F (180°C). Butter the loaf pan and line the bottom with parchment paper. Sift the flour and baking powder together into a bowl. Add the butter and use your fingertips to rub it in until the mixture resembles bread crumbs. Stir in the sugar.

2 Mash the bananas with a fork—you should have 1 cup. Add the bananas, yogurt, and eggs to the flour mixture and stir until combined. Stir in the walnuts. Spread in the pan.

3 Bake about 1 hour 15 minutes, or until a wooden toothpick inserted in the center comes out clean. Transfer to a wire cake rack and let cool 5 minutes. Invert onto the rack, remove the paper, and cool completely.

PREPARE AHEAD Will keep for at least 1 week in an airtight container.

serves 8–10

prep 15 mins
• cook 1 hr 15 mins

9 x 5in (23 x 13cm) loaf pan

Honey loaf

Slice into this sweet loaf cake with the delicate taste of honey.

INGREDIENTS

1 cup butter, room temperature
$^2/_3$ cup light brown sugar (packed)
$^1/_3$ cup plus 1 tbsp honey, warmed until fluid
4 large eggs, lightly beaten
$3^1/_4$ cups all-purpose flour
$1^1/_2$ tsp baking powder
1 tsp ground cinnamon

For the icing

$^2/_3$ cup confectioner's sugar
1 tbsp honey
1–2 tbsp hot water

METHOD

1 Preheat the oven to 350°F (180°C). Butter a 9 x 5in (23 x 13cm) loaf pan and line the bottom with parchment paper.

2 To make the cake, beat the butter and brown sugar with an electric mixer or wooden spoon until pale and creamy. Beat in the honey. One at a time, beat in the eggs, beating well after each addition. Add a little flour if the mixture begins to curdle.

3 Sift together the flour, baking powder, and cinnamon. Stir into the butter mixture. Spread in the pan and smooth the top. Bake for 50–60 minutes, or until a wooden toothpick inserted in the center comes out clean. If the loaf is browning too quickly, tent with foil. Cool in the pan on a wire rack for 10 minutes. Invert and unmold onto the rack, peel off the paper, and let cool.

4 To make the icing, mix the confectioner's sugar and honey, then stir in enough hot water to make a fluid icing. Drizzle the icing over the cake, letting it drip down the sides.

serves 10–12

prep 20 mins,
plus cooling
• cook 60 mins

9 x 5in (23 x
13cm) loaf pan

Lemon, lime, and poppy seed cake

Poppy seeds add a delicate texture to this citrusy loaf cake.

INGREDIENTS

³/₄ cup butter, at room temperature
1 cup granulated sugar
3 large eggs, lightly beaten
finely grated zest of 1 lemon
finely grated zest of 1 lime
2 tbsp fresh lemon juice
1²/₃ cups self-rising flour
2 tbsp poppy seeds
1 tbsp fresh lime juice
1 cup confectioner's sugar

METHOD

1 Preheat the oven to 350°F (180°C). Line the bottom and sides of the loaf pan with parchment paper. In a large bowl, beat the butter and granulated sugar with an electric mixer or wooden spoon until light and fluffy. Gradually beat in the eggs until blended. Fold in the lemon zest, lime zest, and 1 tablespoon of the lemon juice. Sift in the flour, then fold into the batter with the poppy seeds.

2 Scrape into the prepared pan and smooth the top. Bake for 1 hour or until risen, golden, and firm to the touch. Let cool in the pan for 5 minutes, then unmold onto a wire rack and leave to cool completely.

3 Mix the remaining lemon juice with the lime juice in a saucepan. Sift in the confectioner's sugar and whisk over low heat to make a runny glaze. Place parchment paper under the rack to catch the drips, then spoon the warm glaze over the cake, letting it drizzle down the sides. Leave to set before serving.

serves 8–10

prep 15 mins
• cook 1 hr

9 x 5in
(23 x 13cm)
loaf pan

freeze, before
icing, for up to
3 months

Caribbean tea bread

With its flavors of the Caribbean, this is the perfect, satisfying cake to serve with an afternoon cup of tea.

INGREDIENTS

2 teabags
$^2/_3$ cup mixed dried fruit
$^1/_3$ cup dried pineapple, cut into small pieces
$^1/_3$ cup dried mango, cut into small pieces
3 tbsp white rum
$^1/_2$ cup dark brown sugar (packed)
2 large eggs, beaten
$^1/_2$ cup unsalted butter, softened
$^1/_4$ tsp apple pie spice blend or ground cinnamon
2 cups self-rising flour

METHOD

1 To make the tea, pour 1 cup boiling water over the teabags in a heatproof bowl. Leave for 3 minutes, then remove the teabags, squeeze them out into the bowl, and discard.

2 Place the mixed dried fruit, pineapple, and mango in a large bowl, and add the hot tea and rum. Leave to cool to room temperature, then stir and cover with plastic wrap. Leave to macerate for at least 8 hours or overnight.

3 The next day, preheat the oven to 325°F (170°C). Lightly grease the loaf pan and line with parchment paper.

4 Add the sugar, eggs, butter, and spice blend to the fruit, tea, and rum mix. Sift the flour over, and mix until blended. The batter should have a slightly wet consistency.

5 Transfer the batter to the prepared tin and bake for $1^1/_4$ hours, or until a skewer inserted into the center comes out clean. Remove from the oven and leave to cool in the pan for 20 minutes, then turn out onto a wire rack to cool completely.

PREPARE AHEAD The bread keeps for up to 2 days in an airtight container.

serves 6

prep 20 mins, plus cooling
• cook 1 hr 15 mins

macerate for 8 hrs or overnight

8½ x 4½in (21 x 9cm) loaf pan

freeze for up to 3 months

Banana, cranberry, and walnut loaf

Cranberries and walnuts are a delicious combination in this moist loaf.

INGREDIENTS

$^1/_2$ cup unsalted butter, softened
$^3/_4$ cup superfine sugar
2 large eggs, beaten
1 tsp milk
$2^1/_2$ cups all-purpose flour
$^1/_2$ tsp salt
1 tsp baking soda
1 tsp apple pie spice blend
3 bananas, peeled and mashed
$^1/_2$ cup dried cranberries
$^1/_2$ cup walnuts, roughly chopped

METHOD

1 Preheat the oven to 325°F (170°C). Grease 2 small loaf pans and line with parchment paper.

2 Beat the butter and sugar together in a large bowl until pale and creamy. Add the beaten eggs and milk, and mix well.

3 Stir in the flour, salt, baking soda, and spice blend, followed by the bananas, cranberries, and walnuts.

4 Divide the batter between the loaf pans. Bake in the center of the oven for 45–50 minutes. The loaf is cooked when a skewer inserted into the center comes out clean. Remove from the oven and leave to cool in the pan for 10 minutes, then transfer to a wire rack to cool completely.

PREPARE AHEAD The loaf will keep for up to 1 week in an airtight tin.

serves 8–12

prep
20 mins,
plus cooling
• cook 45–50
mins

2 small loaf
pans: 8$^1/_2$ x
4$^1/_2$ x 2$^1/_2$in
(21 x 9 x 6cm)

freeze for
up to 3 months

Stollen

This sweet, German yeast bread makes a great addition to your holiday baking.

INGREDIENTS

$^1/_2$ cup raisins

$^1/_4$ cup dried currants

$^1/_4$ cup dark rum

$^1/_3$ cup plus 1 tbsp whole milk

$^1/_3$ cup granulated sugar

1$^1/_4$oz (7g) packet active dry yeast

3 cups unbleached flour, as needed

$^3/_4$ cup butter, at room temperature

2 large eggs

$^1/_2$ tsp pumpkin pie spice blend

1 tsp pure vanilla extract

$^3/_4$ tsp salt

$^1/_2$ cup mixed candied fruit peel

$^3/_4$ cup chopped slivered almonds

confectioner's sugar, for dusting

METHOD

1 Combine the raisins, currants, and rum in a bowl. Let stand at least 2 hours to plump.

2 Mix the milk and 1 tsp of the granulated sugar in a small bowl. Sprinkle in the yeast and let stand 5 minutes, until softened. Stir to dissolve the yeast. Add $^1/_3$ cup of flour and stir well. Cover with plastic wrap and let stand until doubled in volume, about 30 minutes.

3 Scrape the yeast mixture into the bowl of a heavy-duty mixer. Add the butter, eggs, remaining sugar, pumpkin-pie spice, vanilla, and salt. Mix on low speed with the paddle attachment. Gradually add the remaining flour to make a soft dough that pulls away from the sides of the bowl. Switch to the kneading hook and knead on medium speed until the dough is supple, about 8 minutes. Shape the dough into a ball.

4 Butter a large bowl. Add the dough and turn to coat with butter. Cover with plastic wrap. Let stand in a warm place until doubled in volume, about 1$^1/_4$ hours.

5 Punch the dough. Transfer to a work surface and stretch into a 12 x 10in (30 x 25cm) rectangle. Drain the raisins and currants. Sprinkle the drained fruit, candied fruit peel, and almonds over the dough. Roll and knead to distribute the fruit and almonds, kneading in a bit more flour if needed. Cover and let stand for 10 minutes.

6 Line a baking sheet with parchment paper. Roll out the dough on a lightly floured surface into a 12 x 10in (30 x 25cm) rectangle. Fold one long side over just beyond the middle, then fold over the other long side to overlap the first, curling it over slightly on top to create the traditional "swaddling" shape. Transfer to the baking sheet, cover with plastic wrap, and let stand a warm place about 45 minutes, or until doubled in volume.

7 Preheat the oven to 325°F (170°C). Bake the stollen for about 50 minutes, or until pale golden brown. Sift a generous amount of confectioner's sugar over it. Transfer to a wire cake rack and cool completely. Serve in thick slices.

GOOD WITH Other sweet festive treats, such as marzipan candies.

makes 1 loaf

prep 35 mins, plus soaking, resting, and rising

• cook 50 mins

soak the raisins and currants overnight

freeze, before dusting the top, for up to 1 month

Double chocolate brownies

Proving that two types of chocolate are always better than one, these brownies are rich, moist, and toothsome.

INGREDIENTS

10oz (300g) 70% dark chocolate, broken into pieces
$^1/_2$ cup unsalted butter
1 cup light brown sugar (packed)
5 tbsp olive oil
3 eggs, beaten
1 tsp pure vanilla extract
$^3/_4$ cup all-purpose flour
$^1/_4$ cup cocoa powder
$^1/_2$ tsp baking powder
$1^1/_2$ cups white chocolate, broken into pieces

METHOD

1 Preheat the oven to 350°F (180°C). Grease a 9in (23cm) square baking pan.

2 Place 7oz (200g) of the dark chocolate and the butter in a heatproof bowl, set it over a saucepan of simmering water, and stir occasionally until melted.

3 Place the butter and chocolate mixture, sugar, olive oil, eggs, and vanilla extract in a large bowl. Sift over the flour, cocoa powder, and baking powder, fold in gently with a metal spoon, then fold in the white chocolate pieces and the remaining dark chocolate pieces.

4 Transfer the mix to the prepared pan and bake for 25–30 minutes, or until set on top and a skewer inserted into the center comes out with some moist crumbs attached. Remove from the oven and leave to cool completely in the pan, then remove from the pan and cut into 16 pieces.

PREPARE AHEAD The brownies will keep for up to 5 days in an airtight container.

makes 16

prep 20 mins
• cook 30 mins

9in (23cm)
square
baking pan
• metal spoon
• wooden
skewer

freeze for
up to 3 months

White chocolate and macadamia nut blondies

This white chocolate version of the ever-popular brownie is dotted with silky-textured macadamia nuts.

INGREDIENTS

10oz (300g) white chocolate, chopped
$^3/_4$ cup butter, cubed
$1^1/_2$ cups granulated sugar
4 large eggs
2 cups all-purpose flour
1 cup unsalted macadamia nuts, coarsely chopped

METHOD

1 Preheat the oven to 400°F (200°C). Line the bottom and sides of a 9 x 13in (23 x 33cm) baking pan with parchment paper. In a bowl set over a saucepan of barely simmering water, melt the chocolate and butter together, stirring occasionally until smooth. Remove the bowl and set aside to cool for about 20 minutes.

2 Mix in the sugar (the mixture may become very thick and grainy, but the eggs will loosen it). Using a wire whisk, stir in the eggs one at a time, making sure each is well incorporated before adding the next. Gradually sift in the flour, fold it in, and then stir in the nuts. Scrape the mixture into the prepared pan, gently spreading it into the corners. Bake for 20 minutes, or until just firm to the touch on top but still soft underneath. Place the pan on a wire rack to cool completely, then cut into squares.

makes 24

prep 25 mins
• cook 20 mins

9 x 13in
(23 x 33cm)
rectangular
baking pan

Toffee brownies

These attractively decorated brownies would be perfect for a children's party.

INGREDIENTS

5$^{1}/_{2}$oz (150g) semisweet chocolate, broken into pieces
$^{3}/_{4}$ cup unsalted butter
1$^{1}/_{2}$ cups superfine sugar
4 large eggs
2 tsp pure vanilla extract
1$^{3}/_{4}$ cups all-purpose flour
1 tsp baking powder
1 cup pecans, roughly chopped
7oz (200g) creamy toffee candy
5 tbsp heavy cream

METHOD

1 Preheat the oven to 350°F (180°C). Line the base of the baking pan with parchment paper.

2 Place 3$^{1}/_{2}$oz (100g) of the chocolate in a large heatproof bowl with the butter. Set the bowl over a saucepan of simmering water and stir occasionally until the chocolate has melted and the butter is well combined. Remove from the heat, then stir the sugar into the melted chocolate mix.

3 Lightly beat the eggs with the vanilla in another bowl, then stir them into the chocolate mix. Sift the flour and baking powder into the mixture, fold in lightly with a metal spoon, then fold in the pecans.

4 Place the toffee candy and heavy cream in a saucepan over a gentle heat and stir continuously until melted.

5 Transfer $^{1}/_{2}$ of the chocolate mix to the baking pan and spoon over $^{3}/_{4}$ of the toffee sauce. Spread the rest of the chocolate mix on top and bake for 40–45 minutes, or until firm to the touch. Remove from the oven, leave to cool in the pan for 20 minutes, then turn out onto a wire rack to cool completely, removing the parchment paper for cooling.

6 Decorate by reheating the remaining toffee sauce. Place the remaining chocolate in a small heatproof bowl, set the bowl over a saucepan of simmering water, and stir until the chocolate has melted. Drizzle the toffee sauce over the brownie, followed by the melted chocolate. Leave to cool, then cut into 18 pieces.

PREPARE AHEAD The brownies will keep in an airtight container for up to 5 days.

makes 18

prep 30 mins
• cook 40–45 mins

11 x 7in
(28 x 18cm)
shallow
baking pan

freeze for
up to 3 months

Oatmeal bars

These chewy bars can be made with only a few pantry ingredients.

INGREDIENTS

1 cup butter, plus more for the pan
1 cup light brown sugar (packed)
2 tbsp light corn syrup
3$\frac{1}{2}$ cups rolled (old-fashioned) oats

METHOD

1 Preheat the oven to 300°F (150°C). Lightly butter a 9in (23cm) square baking pan.

2 Heat the butter, brown sugar, and syrup in a large saucepan and stir over medium-low heat until the butter has melted. Remove from the heat and stir in the oats.

3 Spread evenly in the pan. Bake for 40 minutes, or until evenly golden and just beginning to brown at the edges.

4 Transfer to a wire rack and let cool 10 minutes. Cut into bars and let cool completely.

PREPARE AHEAD Make these a few days in advance and store in an airtight container.

makes 16–20

prep 15 mins
• cook 40 mins

9in (23cm) square
baking pan

Sticky date bar cookies

These delicious bars with a gooey layer of dates are ideal for lunchboxes.

INGREDIENTS

2 cups pitted dates (preferably Medjool), chopped

$1/2$ tsp baking soda

$1^1/2$ cups rolled oats

1 cup all-purpose flour

$1/2$ cup light brown sugar (packed)

$1/2$ tsp salt

2 tbsp Lyle's Golden Syrup or light corn syrup

$3/4$ cup butter, cut into pieces

METHOD

1 Preheat the oven to 350°F (180°C). Line the bottom of an 8in (20cm) square baking pan with parchment paper. Place the dates and baking soda in a saucepan with enough water to cover, simmer for 5 minutes, then drain, reserving the liquid. Purée the dates in a blender with 3 tablespoons of the cooking liquid, then set aside.

2 In a bowl, combine the oats, flour, brown sugar, and salt. Add the butter and syrup. Blend the ingredients until the mixture resembles coarse crumbs. Press half of the mixture onto the bottom of the pan. Spread the date purée evenly over the top, then spoon in the remaining oat mixture in an even layer to cover the dates. Bake for 45–55 minutes, or until golden brown. Let cool for 10 minutes, then mark into 16 squares with a knife. Leave to cool completely before removing the cookies with a spatula.

makes 16

prep 25 mins
• cook 45–55 mins

8in (20cm)
square baking pan
• blender

Sticky toffee shortbread

Shortbread becomes utterly addictive when topped with rich chocolate and sticky toffee.

INGREDIENTS

1 cup unsalted butter, at room temperature
$^3/_4$ cup granulated sugar
2 cups all-purpose flour
$^3/_4$ cup semolina (cream of wheat)
4–5 tbsp ready-made toffee sauce
$5^1/_2$oz (150g) cups dark chocolate, broken into pieces
$5^1/_2$oz (150g) white chocolate, broken into pieces

METHOD

1 Preheat the oven to 300°F (150°C). Lightly grease the pan and line with parchment paper. To make the shortbread, beat the butter and sugar together until pale and creamy, then add the flour and semolina, and mix until well combined. Press the mix into the prepared pan, and level the surface with a knife.

2 Bake in the oven for 40–45 minutes, or until lightly golden, then remove and leave it to cool. Spoon the toffee sauce evenly over the shortbread, and smooth the surface with the back of a spoon until level.

3 In two separate heatproof bowls, each set over a pan of simmering water, melt the dark and white chocolate. Spoon blobs of dark and white chocolate randomly over the toffee sauce layer, and create a marbled effect by blending them slightly with the end of a spoon. Refrigerate for a couple of hours for the chocolate to set. Remove from the pan, place on a cutting board, and cut into 24 small squares with a large knife.

makes 24

prep 20 mins, plus chilling • cook 45–50 mins

allow 2 hrs for chilling

8 x 8 x 1½in (20 x 20 x 4cm) square baking pan • large knife

Mocha slice

These crumbly shortbread slices with a rich, dark topping have just a whisper of coffee flavor.

INGREDIENTS

10oz (300g) shortbread cookies
$^2/_3$ cup unsalted butter
$3^1/_2$oz (100g) dark chocolate,
    broken into small pieces
$3^1/_2$oz (100g) coffee-flavored chocolate,
    broken into small pieces
3 large eggs
$^1/_2$ cup superfine sugar
1 tbsp cocoa powder

METHOD

1 Preheat the oven to 375°F (190°C). Grease the tart pan and line with parchment paper.

2 Place the shortbread cookies in a large plastic bag and seal. Hit the bag with the side of a rolling pin until the cookies are crushed into crumbs. Melt half the butter in a medium-sized saucepan, then remove from the heat, and add the crushed cookies. Stir well, until the crumbs are completely coated in the butter, then spread the mix on to the base of the prepared pan, pressing it firmly into the edges of the pan. Set aside.

3 Melt the dark and coffee-flavored chocolate with the remaining butter, in a small heatproof bowl set over a pan of simmering water, stirring occasionally. Then remove the bowl and set aside to cool slightly.

4 Whisk together the eggs and sugar in a large bowl for about 5–8 minutes, until thick and creamy, then fold in the melted chocolate. Pour the mix over the biscuit base. Bake for about 10–15 minutes, until the top forms a crust. Remove and leave to cool completely in the pan. Sprinkle with cocoa powder, and slice into 8 rectangular slices to serve.

GOOD WITH Cherries or raspberries, and some pouring cream.

makes 8

prep 20 mins
• cook 10–15
mins

8 x 11½in
(20 x 29cm)
rectangular
tart pan
with a
removable
bottom

Cherry oat bars

These upmarket granola bars have the perfect texture, and the oats give them a delicious toasty flavor.

INGREDIENTS

$^3/_4$ cup unsalted butter
$^1/_3$ cup light brown sugar (packed)
2 tbsp light corn syrup
3 cups rolled oats
generous $^1/_2$ cup candied cherries, quartered,
    or $^1/_2$ cup dried cherries, roughly chopped
$^1/_3$ cup raisins
$3^1/_2$oz (100g) milk or white chocolate,
    broken into small pieces, to decorate

METHOD

1 Preheat the oven to 350°F (180°C). Lightly grease the cake pan.

2 Place the butter, sugar, and light corn syrup in a medium saucepan over a low heat, and stir until the butter and sugar have melted. Remove the saucepan from the heat, add the oats, cherries, and raisins, and stir until well mixed. Transfer the mix to the prepared pan and press down.

3 Bake at the top of the oven for 25 minutes. Remove from the oven, allow to cool slightly in the pan, then mark into 18 pieces with a knife.

4 When the block of oat bars is cold, place the chocolate in a small heatproof bowl, set it over a saucepan of simmering water, and stir occasionally until the chocolate has melted. Drizzle the melted chocolate over the oat bars, then chill for about 10 minutes, or until the chocolate has set.

5 Remove the block of oat bars from the pan and cut into pieces as marked.

PREPARE AHEAD The bars can be kept in an airtight container for up to 1 week.

makes 18

prep 20 mins,
plus chilling
• cook 25 mins

8 x 8 x 1½in
(20 x 20 x 4cm)
baking pan

Florentine slices

Cut into slices, these yummy treats are a great variation on traditional round Florentines.

INGREDIENTS

8oz (225g) semisweet chocolate,
  broken into pieces
$1/4$ cup unsalted butter
$1/2$ cup demerara sugar
1 egg, beaten
$1/3$ cup mixed dried fruit
1 cup shredded coconut (unsweetened)
$1/4$ cup chopped mixed peel
  or candied cherries

METHOD

1 Grease the cake pan and line with parchment paper.

2 Place the chocolate in a small heatproof bowl, set it over a saucepan of simmering water, and stir occasionally until the chocolate has melted. Spoon the melted chocolate into the prepared cake pan, and spread it evenly over the base. Refrigerate while you make the Florentine mix.

3 Preheat the oven to 300°F (150°C). Place the butter and sugar in a large bowl and cream together until light and fluffy. Beat in the egg.

4 Mix the remaining ingredients in a separate bowl, then add them to the butter mixture. Stir well to ensure the fruit is evenly distributed, then spoon the batter over the set chocolate in the pan.

5 Bake in the center of the oven for 40–45 minutes, or until golden brown. Remove from the oven and leave to stand in the pan for 5 minutes.

6 Mark out 16 squares using a sharp knife, but make sure you do not cut into the chocolate—it is still runny and if your knife touches it, the sides of the squares will be smeared with chocolate. Leave until completely cold, then cut right through, loosen each square with a knife, and remove carefully from the pan.

PREPARE AHEAD The slices can be stored in an airtight container for up to 1 week.

makes 16

prep 20 mins
• cook 40–45 mins

8 x 8 x 2in (20 x 20 x 5cm) baking pan

Panforte

This famous cake from Siena, Italy, dates from the 13th century.

INGREDIENTS

edible rice (wafer) paper (available online at cake suppliers),
  for lining, or well-oiled parchment paper
1 cup whole blanched almonds, toasted and roughly chopped
1 cup hazelnuts, toasted, skinned, and roughly chopped
$^2/_3$ cup chopped candied orange peel
$^2/_3$ cup chopped candied lemon peel
1 cup coarsely chopped dried figs
$^1/_2$ cup rice or all-purpose flour
finely grated zest of 1 lemon
$^1/_2$ tsp ground cinnamon
$^1/_2$ tsp freshly grated nutmeg
$^1/_4$ tsp ground cloves
$^1/_4$ tsp ground allspice
$^2/_3$ cup sugar
$^1/_4$ cup honey
2 tbsp butter, plus more for the pan
confectioner's sugar, for sifting

METHOD

1 Preheat the oven to 350°F (180°C). Butter an 8in (20cm) springform pan. Line the bottom and sides of the pan with parchment paper. Place a round of rice paper in the bottom of the pan.

2 Stir the almonds, hazelnuts, candied peels, figs, rice flour, lemon zest, cinnamon, nutmeg, cloves, and allspice together in a bowl.

3 Stir the sugar, honey, and butter in a small saucepan over low heat until melted. Pour into the nut mixture and stir well. Spoon into the pan, and with moistened hands, press until smooth and even.

4 Bake for 30 minutes, until set. Transfer to a wire rack and let cool completely in the pan. Remove the sides of the pan and invert onto the rack. Peel off the parchment but leave the rice paper in place. Turn right side up.

5 Sift confectioner's sugar over the panforte. Slice into thin wedges and serve.

PREPARE AHEAD You can make this up to 3 days in advance, and store it in an airtight container.

serves 12–16

prep 30 mins
• cook 30 mins

8in (20cm)
springform
cake
pan

Apricot crumble shortbread

This is a fruity twist on plain shortbread with a sweet, textured topping.

INGREDIENTS

$^1/_2$ cup butter, at room temperature
$^1/_4$ cup granulated sugar
$^3/_4$ cup plus 2 tbsp all-purpose flour
6 tbsp cornstarch
1 x 15–16oz (410g) can apricot halves,
    drained and coarsely chopped

For the topping

2 tbsp butter, cubed
$^3/_4$ cup all-purpose flour
3 tbsp raw or granulated sugar

METHOD

1 Beat together the butter and sugar with an electric mixer or wooden spoon until pale and creamy. Sift in the flour and cornstarch and combine so that the mixture forms a dough. (You'll probably need to use your hands at the end.) Knead the dough lightly until smooth, then press evenly onto the bottom and halfway up the sides of the pan. Refrigerate for at least 1 hour or until firm.

2 Preheat the oven to 350°F (180°C). Make the topping by rubbing the cubed butter into the flour in a bowl with your fingertips until the mixture resembles coarse bread crumbs. Stir in the sugar. Scatter the apricots evenly over the chilled dough, then top with the crumb mixture, pressing down gently so that it is packed on. Place the pan on a baking sheet and bake for 45 minutes, or until the shortbread is lightly browned at the edges and the topping is just golden. Transfer to a wire rack to cool for 15 minutes, then lift off the edge of the pan and allow to cool completely. Cut the shortbread into bars or squares.

makes 10 bars,
or 20 squares

prep 20 mins,
plus chilling and
cooling
• cook 45 mins

13¾ x 4½in
(35 x 11cm) pan
with removable
bottom

Raspberry, lemon, and almond bake

Sweet almond cake topped with tart raspberries is a moreish treat.

INGREDIENTS

1¼ cups all-purpose flour
1 tsp baking powder
1 cup ground almonds
½ cup plus 3 tbsp butter, cubed
1 cup granulated sugar
3 tbsp fresh lemon juice
1 tsp pure vanilla extract
2 large eggs
1 cup fresh raspberries
confectioner's sugar,
    for dusting (optional)

METHOD

1 Preheat the oven to 350°F (180°C). Line the bottom and sides of an 8in (20cm) square baking pan with parchment paper. Sift the flour and baking powder into a bowl, and stir in the ground almonds. In a small saucepan, heat the butter, sugar, and lemon juice together, stirring until melted and smooth. Let cool slightly.

2 Stir the syrupy butter mixture into the dry ingredients, then mix in the vanilla extract and the eggs, one at a time, until the mixture is smooth and well blended. Scrape into the prepared pan, then scatter the raspberries over the top. Bake for 35–40 minutes or until golden and a skewer inserted into the cake comes out clean.

3 Cool in the pan for 10 minutes, then unmold and cool completely on a wire rack. Just before serving, dust with confectioner's sugar. To serve, cut into squares or bars.

serves 8

prep 20 mins,
plus cooling
• cook 40 mins

8 x 8 x 2in
(20 x 20 x
5cm) square
baking
pan

freeze for
up to 2 months

Toffee apple bake

Bake this on a winter evening and serve warm for a special treat.

INGREDIENTS

2 medium Granny Smith apples, peeled, cored, and thinly sliced
squeeze of lemon juice
$3^{1}/_{4}$ cups self-rising flour
2 tsp baking powder
2 cups light brown sugar (packed)
4 large eggs, lightly beaten
1 cup butter, melted
1 tbsp granulated sugar

For the toffee sauce

$^{1}/_{2}$ cup butter
$^{2}/_{3}$ cup light brown sugar (packed)
1 tbsp fresh lemon juice
sea salt
crème fraîche, to serve (optional)

METHOD

1 Preheat the oven to 350°F (180°C). Line the bottom and sides of a 13 x 9in (33 x 23cm) baking pan with parchment paper. Put the apple slices in a bowl and toss with the lemon juice to prevent browning.

2 Sift the flour and baking powder into a large mixing bowl, and stir in the brown sugar. Beat in the eggs and the melted butter with an electric mixer or wooden spoon to make a smooth batter. Pour into the prepared pan and smooth the top. Arrange the apple slices in three or four rows on top of the batter and sprinkle with the sugar. Bake for 45 minutes, or until the cake is firm to the touch and a skewer inserted into the center comes out clean.

3 Meanwhile, make the sauce by melting the butter and sugar in a saucepan over medium-low heat. Add the lemon juice and a pinch of salt, whisking until the mixture is melted and smooth. Let cool slightly. Pour the sauce over the cake while it is still in the pan, gently brushing over the top. Serve warm or at room temperature, with a dollop of crème fraîche.

makes 18
squares

prep 20 mins
• cook 45 mins

13 x 9in
(33 x 23cm)
rectangular
baking pan

White chocolate cakes

These delicious cakes are studded with crunchy walnuts.

INGREDIENTS
$^1/_4$ cup butter, softened
$^1/_4$ cup superfine sugar
1 tsp pure vanilla extract
2 eggs, lightly beaten
$^3/_4$ cup self-rising flour
7oz (200g) white chocolate, finely chopped
1 cup walnuts, chopped

For the topping
7oz (200g) white chocolate
$^1/_2$ cup walnuts, chopped, to decorate

METHOD
1 Preheat the oven to 325°F (170°C). Grease a high-sided 8in (20cm) square baking pan with butter. Line with parchment paper and set it aside.

2 Cream the butter, sugar, and vanilla extract in a bowl with a handheld electric mixer or wooden spoon until pale and creamy. Add the eggs a little at a time, beating well after each addition. Gently fold in the flour, then the chocolate and the chopped walnuts.

3 Spread the mixture in the pan and smooth the top. Bake for 25–30 minutes, or until set. Cool in the pan for 10 minutes before turning out onto a wire rack to cool.

4 For the topping, melt the white chocolate in a heatproof bowl placed over gently simmering water, stirring, until smooth and glossy. Spread it evenly over the cooled cake. Allow it to set, then decorate with chopped walnuts, and cut it into 9 squares.

makes 9

prep 10 mins
• cook 25–30 mins

8 x 8 x 2in
(20 x 20 x 5cm)
baking pan

Chocolate cookie torte

Crunchy, chocolatey, and sweet, this no-bake cake couldn't be easier to make.

INGREDIENTS

$^3/_4$ cup butter, cut into pieces
9oz (250g) semisweet chocolate, broken into pieces
2 tbsp Lyle's Golden Syrup or light corn syrup
1lb (450g) graham crackers, coarsely crushed
handful of plump golden raisins
handful of natural almonds, coarsely chopped

METHOD

1 Lightly grease an 8in (20cm) square baking pan. In a large saucepan, combine the butter, chocolate, and syrup. Cook over low heat, stirring, for 5–10 minutes, or until melted and smooth. Remove from the heat and stir in the graham crackers, raisins, and almonds. Mix well, then press the mixture into the pan with the back of a spoon. Refrigerate for at least 2 hours to solidify the cake.

serves 6

prep 10 mins

allow at least 2 hrs for chilling

8 x 8 x 2in (20 x 20 x 5cm) baking pan

SMALL BAKES & MUFFINS

Madeleines

These little treats were made famous by writer Marcel Proust.

INGREDIENTS

1/4 cup butter, melted, and cooled until tepid, plus more for the pan
1/3 cup plus 2 tbsp all-purpose flour
1/3 cup plus 1 tbsp sugar
2 large eggs, at room temperature
1 tsp pure vanilla extract
1/4 tsp baking powder
1/8 tsp salt
confectioner's sugar, to garnish

METHOD

1 Preheat the oven to 350°F (180°C). Carefully brush the indentations of the madeleine pan with melted butter. Dust with flour and tap to remove the excess.

2 Beat the sugar, eggs, and vanilla with a wire whisk or an electric mixer on high speed for 4 minutes, until the mixture triples in volume and forms a ribbon when the beaters are lifted.

3 Sift the flour, baking powder, and salt together twice. Sift the flour mixture over the egg mixture. Pour the butter down the inside of the bowl. Using a spatula, fold gently together, keeping the batter light and airy. Spoon the batter into the molds.

4 Bake for 12 minutes, or until golden. Unmold and cool completely. Sift confectioner's sugar over the tops just before serving.

makes 12

prep 15–20
mins
• cook 12 mins

madeleine pan
or 12-hole
muffin pan

freeze for
up to 1 month

French almond financiers

These cakes are so-named because they are said to resemble gold bars.

INGREDIENTS

6 tbsp butter, softened, plus more for the molds
3 tbsp all-purpose flour, plus more for the molds
$^{1}/_{2}$ cup ground almonds
$^{3}/_{4}$ cup confectioner's sugar, sifted
pinch of salt
3 large egg whites
$^{1}/_{2}$ tsp pure vanilla extract

METHOD

1 Preheat the oven to 400°F (200°C). Butter and flour 12 financier or barquette molds (available at specialty kitchenware stores). Place on a baking sheet, if necessary.

2 Mix the almonds, sugar, and salt together. Heat the butter over low heat, just until melted. Whisk the egg whites until they are frothy but barely thickened. Add the butter, egg whites, and vanilla extract to the dry ingredients and fold together.

3 Divide the batter among the molds, filling halfway. Bake for about 12 minutes, or until they spring back when pressed lightly. Cool briefly, remove from the molds onto a wire rack, and cool completely.

makes 12

prep 15 mins
• cook
12 mins

12 financier
molds or
barquette molds,
or a 12-hole
muffin pan

freeze for
up to 3 months

Nutty date muffins

These British-style buns are great for the lunchbox or as an after-school treat.

INGREDIENTS

1$\frac{1}{2}$ cups self-rising flour
$\frac{1}{3}$ cup cream of wheat or ground rice
$\frac{1}{2}$ cup unsalted butter, cut in small pieces
$\frac{1}{3}$ cup granulated sugar
$\frac{2}{3}$ cup pitted dried dates, finely chopped
$\frac{1}{2}$ cup walnuts, chopped
2 large eggs, beaten
1 tsp pure vanilla extract
12 walnut halves, to decorate

For the icing
1 tbsp instant coffee granules
$\frac{2}{3}$ cup confectioner's sugar

METHOD

1 Grease a 12-cup muffin pan. Preheat the oven to 375°F (190°C). Place the flour and cream of wheat or ground rice in a large bowl, then add the butter and rub in. Stir in the sugar, dates, and walnuts. Add the eggs and vanilla extract, and mix to a stiff consistency.

2 Spoon the mixture into the bun tray and bake toward the top of the oven for approximately 10–12 minutes. Remove from the oven and leave to cool in the pan for 10 minutes, then transfer to a wire rack for icing.

3 Make the icing by mixing the instant coffee granules with 1 tbsp boiling water. Blend the coffee solution with the confectioner's sugar until the icing is of a dropping consistency.

4 Drizzle the icing over each bun using a teaspoon, then top with half a walnut and leave the icing to set.

makes 12

prep 15 mins
• cook 12 mins

eat on the day
of making

12-cup
standard
muffin pan

Petit fours

Gorgeous to look at and gorgeous to eat, these are perfect party cakes.

INGREDIENTS
3/4 cup unsalted butter, softened
3/4 cup superfine sugar
3 large eggs
1 tsp pure vanilla extract
1 1/2 cups self-rising flour
2 tbsp milk
2–3 tbsp raspberry or red cherry preserves
royal icing flowers, to decorate (optional)

For the buttercream
1/3 cup unsalted butter, softened
1 cup confectioner's sugar, sifted

For the frosting
juice of 1/2 lemon
2 2/3 cups confectioner's sugar
1–2 drops pink food coloring

METHOD

1 Preheat the oven to 375°F (190°C). Grease the cake pan and line with parchment paper. Place the butter and sugar in a large bowl and beat until pale and fluffy. Set aside.

2 Lightly beat the eggs and vanilla extract in another large bowl. Add about 1/4 of the egg mix and 1 tablespoon of the flour to the butter mix and beat well, then add the rest of the egg, a little at a time, beating as you go. Sift over the rest of the flour, add the milk, and fold in with a metal spoon.

3 Transfer the batter to the prepared cake pan and bake in the center of the oven for about 25 minutes, or until lightly golden and springy to the touch. Remove from the oven, leave to cool in the pan for about 10 minutes, then remove from the pan and cool upside down on a wire rack.

4 To make the buttercream, beat the butter with the confectioner's sugar until the mixture is smooth. Set aside.

5 Slice the cake horizontally and spread the fruit preserves on one half and the buttercream on the other. Sandwich together, then cut into 16 equal squares.

6 To make the frosting, put the lemon juice in a measuring jug and make it up to 2fl oz (60ml) with hot water. Mix this with the confectioner's sugar, stirring continuously and adding more hot water as required until the mixture is smooth. Add 1–2 drops pink food coloring and stir well.

7 Stand the cakes on a wire rack set over a board or plate (to catch the drips), then drizzle with the frosting to cover the cakes completely, or just cover the tops of the cakes and allow the frosting to drip down the sides so the sponge layers are visible.

8 Decorate with royal icing flowers (if using), then leave to set for about 15 minutes. Use a clean palette knife to transfer each cake carefully to a paper case.

PREPARE AHEAD Store the frosted petit fours on a tray, uncovered, in the refrigerator for up to 1 day.

makes 16

prep 30 mins
• cook 25 mins

8in (20cm)
square cake pan
• paper liners

freeze, unfilled
and without
frosting, for up
to 3 months

Berry friands

Friands are small French-style cakes flavored with almonds.

INGREDIENTS

1 cup confectioner's sugar
7 tbsp all-purpose flour
1 cup ground almonds
3 large egg whites
5 tbsp unsalted butter, melted
1 cup mixed fresh berries, such
   as blueberries and raspberries

METHOD

1 Preheat the oven to 350°F (180°C). Sift the sugar and flour into a bowl, then stir in the ground almonds. In another bowl, whisk the egg whites with an electric mixer or a wire whisk until they form soft peaks.

2 Gently fold the flour mixture and the melted butter into the egg whites until incorporated. Divide the batter equally between six muffin cups lined with paper liners. Scatter the berries evenly over the top of each one, gently pressing them into the batter. Bake for 30–35 minutes, or until golden brown and risen.

makes 6

prep 15 mins
• cook 35 mins

6-cup
muffin pan
• cupcake liners

Lemon poppy seed muffins

Best eaten freshly made, this quick-to-make treat is perfect for brunch.

INGREDIENTS

$2^2/_3$ cups all-purpose flour
$1^1/_2$ tsp baking powder
$^1/_2$ tsp baking soda
$^1/_4$ tsp salt
$^1/_2$ cup granulated sugar
$2^1/_2$ tbsp poppy seeds
2 large eggs
1 cup plus 2 tbsp sour cream
$^1/_4$ cup butter, melted and cooled
$^1/_4$ cup vegetable oil
zest of 2 large lemons, finely grated
confectioner's sugar, for dusting

METHOD

1 Preheat the oven to 400°F (200°C). Line a 12-cup muffin pan with paper liners. Sift the flour, baking powder, baking soda, and salt into a large bowl. Stir in the sugar and poppy seeds, making a well in the center.

2 In a separate bowl, beat the eggs. Stir in the sour cream, butter, oil, and lemon zest. Add to the flour mixture and stir until just mixed. Divide the batter among the muffin cups, filling each one three-quarters full.

3 Bake the muffins for 20 minutes, or until golden brown and a toothpick inserted in the center comes out clean. Remove the muffins from the pan and transfer to a wire rack to cool. Sift confectioner's sugar over the tops while still warm.

makes 12

prep 10 mins
• cook 20 mins

12-cup muffin pan
• cupcake liners

156

Banana and chocolate chip muffins

These nice moist muffins have a good banana flavor and plenty of oozing chocolate.

INGREDIENTS

1 cup all-purpose flour
$1/3$ cup fine cornmeal
1 tsp baking powder
1 tsp baking soda
$1/2$ cup light brown sugar (packed)
3 tbsp unsalted butter, melted
1 egg, beaten
2 bananas, peeled and well mashed
$1/3$ cup buttermilk or plain yogurt
$1/2$ cup milk chocolate chips

METHOD

1 Preheat the oven to 400°F (200°C). Line the muffin pan with 8 paper liners.

2 Sift together the flour, cornmeal, baking powder, and baking soda in a large bowl. Stir in the sugar, then set aside.

3 Place the melted butter, beaten egg, mashed bananas, and buttermilk or yogurt in a separate bowl and mix together. Fold the banana mix gently into the flour mix using a metal spoon, taking care not to overmix. Fold in the chocolate chips.

4 Spoon the mix into the muffin cups, and bake for 20–30 minutes, or until golden brown and firm to the touch. Remove from the oven and leave to cool completely in the pan.

PREPARE AHEAD The muffins keep for up to 1 week in an airtight tin.

makes 8

prep 15 mins
• cook 30 mins

12-cup standard
muffin pan
• cupcake liners

freeze for
up to 3 months

Apple muffins

These are best served straight from the oven for breakfast, but are also good in lunchboxes or as an afternoon snack.

INGREDIENTS

1 Golden Delicious apple, peeled, cored, and diced
$\frac{1}{2}$ cup light brown sugar (packed)
2 tsp lemon juice
$1\frac{1}{3}$ cups all-purpose flour
$\frac{1}{3}$ cup whole wheat flour
4 tsp baking powder
1 tbsp pumpkin-pie spice
$\frac{1}{2}$ tsp salt
$\frac{1}{4}$ cup pecans, coarsely chopped
1 cup whole milk
$\frac{1}{4}$ cup vegetable oil
1 large egg, beaten
turbinado sugar, for sprinkling

METHOD

1 Preheat the oven to 400°F (200°C). Line a 12-cup muffin pan with paper liners. Combine the apple, $\frac{1}{4}$ cup brown sugar, and the lemon juice in a bowl, and mix until the apple pieces are evenly coated. Set aside for 5 minutes.

2 Meanwhile, whisk together the flours, baking powder, pumpkin-pie spice, and salt in a large bowl. Mix in the remaining brown sugar and pecans.

3 Whisk together the milk, oil, and egg, then add the apple mixture. Pour into the dry ingredients and stir until just mixed.

4 Divide the batter among the muffin cups, filling them about two-thirds full. Sprinkle with the turbinado sugar. Bake for 20–25 minutes, until the tops are rounded and light brown. Immediately unmold the muffins onto a wire rack. Serve hot, warm, or at room temperature.

makes 12

prep 10 mins
• cook 20–25
mins

12-cup standard
muffin pan
• cupcake liners

Blueberry muffins

A perennially favorite flavor for muffins, blueberry tastes even better with a hint of lemon.

INGREDIENTS
$2^1/_4$ cups self-rising flour
1 tsp baking powder
6 tbsp granulated sugar
finely grated zest of 1 lemon (optional)
salt
1 cup plain yogurt
2 large eggs, lightly beaten
$3^1/_2$ tbsp butter, melted and cooled slightly
$1^1/_2$ cups blueberries

METHOD
1 Preheat the oven to 400°F (200°C). Line a 12-cup muffin pan with paper liners. Sift the flour and baking powder into a large bowl, then mix in the sugar, lemon zest, and a pinch of salt. Make a well in the center.

2 Mix the yogurt, eggs, and butter in a bowl, then pour into the dry ingredients, along with the blueberries. Fold together lightly, just until combined; don't overmix or the muffins will be heavy. Don't worry if a few lumps remain in the batter.

3 Spoon evenly into the muffin cups and bake for 20 minutes or until risen and golden. Cool in the pan for 5 minutes, then serve warm or let cool to room temperature.

makes 12

prep 15 mins
• cook 20 mins

12-cup
muffin pan
• cupcake liners

Chocolate muffins

These muffins are sure to satisfy chocolate cravings, and the buttermilk lends a delicious lightness.

INGREDIENTS

$1^2/_3$ cups all-purpose flour
$^2/_3$ cup Dutch-process cocoa powder
2 tsp baking powder
$^1/_2$ tsp baking soda
$^1/_4$ tsp salt
$^3/_4$ cup light brown sugar (packed)
1 cup plus 2 tbsp buttermilk
$^1/_3$ cup plus 2 tbsp vegetable oil
2 large eggs
$^1/_2$ tsp pure vanilla extract
1 cup semisweet chocolate chips

METHOD

1 Preheat the oven to 400°F (200°C). Line a 12-cup muffin pan with paper liners.

2 Sift the flour, cocoa powder, baking powder, baking soda, and salt into a large bowl. Stir in the brown sugar, then make a well in the center.

3 Whisk together the buttermilk, oil, eggs, and vanilla. Pour into the well in the flour mixture and stir until the batter is just combined. Fold in the chocolate chips. Divide the batter among the muffin cups, filling each one three-quarters full.

4 Bake for 20 minutes, or until a toothpick inserted in the center comes out clean. Remove the muffins from the pan, transfer to a wire rack, and cool completely.

makes 12

prep 10 mins
• cook 20 mins

12-cup muffin pan
• cupcake liners

Vanilla cupcakes

Colored buttercream frosting and simple decorations transform these humble cupcakes into treats fit for a celebration.

INGREDIENTS

2 cups all-purpose flour
2 tsp baking powder
1¼ cups butter, softened
1½ cups sugar
6 large eggs
1 tsp pure vanilla extract
⅓ cup milk
vanilla buttercream frosting, colored pale pink and yellow
metallic or colored candies, for garnish (optional)

METHOD

1 Preheat the oven to 350°F (180°C). Line a 12-cup muffin pan with paper liners.

2 Sift the flour and baking powder into a bowl. Add the butter, sugar, eggs, vanilla, and milk. Beat with a wooden spoon or an electric mixer for 3 minutes, until pale and fluffy. Divide among the muffin cups. Bake 25–30 minutes, until golden brown. Let cool in the pan, then transfer to a wire rack to cool completely.

3 Pipe a swirl of frosting on top of each cupcake and decorate with the candies, if using.

makes 18–20

prep 15 mins
• cook 30 mins

12-cup standard
muffin pan
• cupcake liners
• pastry bag

Chocolate-frosted cupcakes

Kids will adore the creamy, chocolatey frosting on these dainty cupcakes.

INGREDIENTS

9 tbsp butter, at room temperature
$^2/_3$ cup granulated sugar
2 large eggs
$1^1/_4$ cups self-rising flour, sifted
1 tsp pure vanilla extract
1 tbsp whole milk, if needed

For the frosting

1 cup confectioner's sugar
3 tbsp unsweetened cocoa powder
7 tbsp butter, at room temperature
few drops of pure vanilla extract
2 tbsp whole milk, if needed
dark chocolate, shaved into curls
    with a vegetable peeler (optional)

METHOD

1 Preheat the oven to 375°F (190°C). Line a 12-cup muffin pan with paper liners. Place the butter and sugar in a bowl and beat with an electric mixer or wooden spoon until pale and fluffy. Beat in the eggs one at a time, adding 1 tablespoon of the flour after each addition. Beat in the vanilla extract and then the rest of the flour until smooth and blended—the mixture should drop easily off the beaters or spoon. If it doesn't, stir in the milk. Divide the mixture evenly between the muffin cups. Bake for 20 minutes or until risen, golden, and firm to the touch. Transfer the cupcakes to a wire rack to cool completely.

2 To make the frosting, sift the confectioner's sugar and cocoa powder (if using) into a bowl. Beat in the butter and the vanilla with an electric mixer or wooden spoon until the mixture is light and fluffy. If the frosting is too thick, beat in the milk. Frost the cupcakes, swirling the frosting decoratively. Scatter the dark chocolate shavings over the frosting, if desired.

makes 12

prep 25 mins
• cook 20 mins

12-cup
muffin pan
• cupcake liners

freeze, before
frosting, for up to
3 months

Orange and lemon cupcakes

These pretty cupcakes are great for celebrations.

INGREDIENTS

1 cup unsalted butter
1 cup superfine sugar
3 large eggs
$1^3/_4$ cups self-rising flour
finely grated zest and juice of 1 large orange
finely grated zest of 1 lemon
sugar sprinkles, to decorate

For the buttercream

$^1/_4$ cup unsalted butter
$^3/_4$ cup confectioner's sugar
juice of 1 lemon
few drops of yellow food coloring (optional)
few drops of orange food coloring (optional)

METHOD

1 Preheat the oven to 350°F (180°C). Line the muffin pan with 12 paper liners.

2 Place the butter, sugar, eggs, flour, and orange and lemon zest in a bowl and beat until the mixture is pale and fluffy. Add the orange juice, a little at a time, until the batter is of a dropping consistency.

3 Spoon the batter into the muffin cups and bake for 25–30 minutes, or until lightly golden brown, risen, and springy to the touch. Remove from the oven and leave to cool in the pan for a few minutes before transferring to a wire rack to cool completely.

4 To make the buttercream, beat the butter and confectioner's sugar together in a small bowl, then stir in the lemon juice. If using food coloring, divide the frosting mixture between two bowls. Mix the yellow coloring into one portion of frosting, a few drops at a time, until you have the desired color, and a few drops of orange into the other portion.

5 Spread the frosting generously over the cakes then decorate with sugar sprinkles.

PREPARE AHEAD The cupcakes can be stored in an airtight container for several days.

makes 12

prep 15 mins
• cook 30 mins

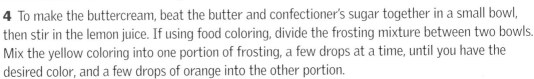

12-cup
muffin pan
• cupcake liners

freeze, without
the frosting, for
up to 3 months

Chocolate chip cupcakes

Children will enjoy decorating these—they can add their favorite sweets to the simple chocolate topping.

INGREDIENTS

1 cup all-purpose flour
1 cup sugar
$^1/_2$ tsp baking soda
$^1/_4$ tsp baking powder
$^1/_4$ tsp salt
$^3/_4$ cup buttermilk
2oz (60g) unsweetened chocolate, melted and tepid
$^1/_4$ cup butter, softened
1 large egg, at room temperature
$^1/_2$ tsp pure vanilla extract
1 cup semisweet chocolate chips

For the topping

$^2/_3$ cup heavy cream
5oz (140g) semisweet chocolate, chopped

METHOD

1 Preheat the oven to 350°F (180°C). Line 2 muffin pans with 15 paper liners. Combine all the ingredients through the vanilla in a bowl. Beat for 3 minutes, until light and fluffy. Stir in the chocolate chips. Divide among the muffin cups. Bake about 20 minutes. Cool completely.

2 Boil the cream. Remove from the heat, add the chocolate, and stir and cool. Dip each cupcake in the chocolate mixture to top.

makes 15

prep 15 mins
• cook 20 mins

12-cup standard
muffin pan
• cupcake liners

Raspberry cupcakes

These elegant cakes are perfect with after-dinner coffee.

INGREDIENTS

1²/₃ cups all-purpose flour
1 cup butter, softened
1 cup sugar
4 large eggs
1 tsp baking powder
1 tsp pure vanilla extract
¹/₂ tsp almond extract
6oz (175g) plus 12 raspberries
3 tbsp finely chopped almonds
6oz (175g) white chocolate, chopped, plus grated, for garnish

METHOD

1 Preheat the oven to 350°F (180°C). Line 12 muffin cups with paper liners.

2 Beat the flour, butter, sugar, eggs, baking powder, vanilla extract, and almond extract in a bowl for 3 minutes, until pale and fluffy. Stir in the raspberries (reserving 12) and almonds. Divide among the muffin cups. Bake for 25–30 minutes, until golden. Cool for 10 minutes; transfer the cupcakes to a wire rack to cool completely.

3 Melt the white chocolate (reserving shavings) in a heatproof bowl set over a saucepan of simmering water. Drizzle over the cupcakes. Top with grated white chocolate and a raspberry.

makes 12

prep 15 mins
• cook 30 mins

12-cup standard
muffin pan
• cupcake liners
• pastry bag

Cinnamon apple and raisin cupcakes

Apples and golden raisins seem made for each other in these delicious, moist cupcakes.

INGREDIENTS

$^1/_2$ cup unsalted butter, softened
$^1/_2$ cup superfine sugar
2 eggs
1 cup self-rising flour
$^1/_2$ tsp baking powder
1 tsp ground cinnamon
3 green eating apples,
   peeled, cored, and grated
$^1/_3$ cup golden raisins

For the frosting

1 cup unsalted butter, softened
$2^2/_3$ cups confectioner's sugar, sifted
2 tbsp lemon juice
ground cinnamon, to dust

METHOD

1 Preheat the oven to 350°F (180°C). Line the muffin pan with 12 paper liners.

2 Put the softened butter, sugar, eggs, flour, baking powder, and cinnamon in a large mixing bowl and beat well for a few minutes until light and fluffy. Add the grated apples and raisins and beat briefly again.

3 Spoon the mix into the muffin cups, and bake for about 15 minutes, or until well risen and golden, and the centers spring back when lightly pressed. Transfer to a wire rack to cool.

4 To make the frosting, beat the softened butter in a bowl. Gradually beat in the confectioner's sugar and lemon juice until soft and fluffy. Pipe or swirl the frosting on top of the cupcakes and dust with cinnamon.

makes 12

prep 15 mins
• cook 15 mins

12-cup
muffin pan
• cupcake liners

Lime drizzle cupcakes

These are equally delicious made with a large lemon instead of the limes.

INGREDIENTS
$1/2$ cup unsalted butter,
   softened
$1/2$ cup superfine sugar
2 eggs
1 cup self-rising flour
$1/2$ tsp baking powder
finely grated zest of 1 lime

For the topping
finely grated zest of 1 lime, or
   zest of 1 lime with $3/4$ finely grated, and $1/4$ thinly pared
   and cut into thin strips, to decorate (optional)
juice of 2 limes (from the fruit used for the zest)
$1/4$ cup superfine sugar

METHOD
1 Preheat the oven to 350°F (180°C). Line the cupcake pan with 12 paper liners. To make the cakes, put the softened butter, sugar, eggs, flour, baking powder, and zest of 1 lime in a large mixing bowl. Beat well with an electric mixer for 2 minutes, or with a wooden spoon for about 3 minutes, until light and fluffy.

2 Spoon the batter into the muffin cups and bake for about 15 minutes, or until well risen and the centers spring back when lightly pressed. Transfer to a wire rack to cool.

3 Meanwhile, for the garnish, boil the strips of lime zest in water for 2 minutes (if using), drain, rinse with cold water, drain again, and set aside.

4 To make the topping, mix the lime juice, grated lime zest, and sugar together. Prick the tops of the cupcakes lightly with a skewer and spoon a little of the mix over each one, catching any surplus syrup in a bowl underneath to drizzle again. Leave to set for a few seconds then repeat until all the topping is used. Decorate by coating the strips of lime zest (if using) with superfine sugar and use to top each cupcake. Leave to cool. The lime juice will sink in, leaving a crusty top.

makes 12

prep 15 mins
• cook 15 mins

12-cup
standard
muffin pan
• cupcake
liners

Strawberry and cream cupcakes

These cupcakes are filled with a fresh strawberry filling and are a luscious treat, and pretty enough for a special dessert.

INGREDIENTS
2 eggs, separated
$1/2$ cup superfine sugar
$1/3$ cup unsalted butter, softened
$3/4$ cup self-rising flour
$1/4$ cup cornstarch
$1/4$ tsp pure vanilla extract

For the filling and topping
8oz (225g) strawberries
$2/3$ cup heavy or whipping cream
2 tbsp superfine sugar
few drops of lemon juice

METHOD

1 Preheat the oven to 400°F (200°C). Line the cupcake pan with 12 paper liners.

2 Whisk the egg whites until stiff, then whisk in 1 tablespoon of the sugar and set aside. Beat the butter and sugar in a mixing bowl with an electric mixer or wooden spoon until light and fluffy. Beat in the egg yolks. Sift the flour and cornstarch over the surface and beat in with 2 tablespoons of hot water plus the vanilla extract. Gently fold in the whisked egg whites with a metal spoon. Do not over mix, but make sure all the egg white is incorporated.

3 Spoon the batter into the muffin cups and bake for about 12 minutes, or until well risen and golden, and the centers spring back when lightly pressed. Transfer to a wire rack to cool.

4 Meanwhile, select 6 small or 3 large strawberries and cut into halves or quarters, including the hulls, and reserve for decoration. Hull and chop the remainder and sweeten to taste with a little of the sugar, and sharpen with a few drops of lemon juice. Whip the cream and the remaining sugar until peaking.

5 Cut out a circle of sponge from each cake so you end up with a small well in the center, leaving a $1/4$in (5mm) border all around. Fill with the chopped strawberries. Pipe or spoon the whipped cream on top, and put a strawberry half or quarter on the top of each. Place the cut out rounds of sponge at an angle to the side of the strawberries and press gently into the cream to secure.

makes 12

**prep 15 mins
• cook 12 mins**

**12-cup
standard
muffin pan
• cupcake
liners**

Blueberry and pistachio angel cupcakes

These look beautiful and taste sublime. Serve as an afternoon snack or dessert.

INGREDIENTS
$1/2$ cup shelled pistachio nuts
2 large egg whites
pinch of salt
$1/2$ tsp cream of tartar
$1/2$ cup superfine sugar
$1/3$ cup all-purpose flour
$1^1/2$ tbsp cornstarch
$1/4$ tsp natural almond extract
$1/4$ tsp pure vanilla extract
$1/2$ cup dried blueberries

For the cream cheese frosting
$2/3$ cup heavy cream
4 tbsp confectioner's sugar
$2/3$ cup cream cheese
a few fresh or dried blueberries (optional)

METHOD

1 Preheat the oven to 325°F (170°C). Line the cupcake pan with 12 paper liners.

2 Put the pistachios in a bowl, cover with boiling water, and leave to stand for 5 minutes. Drain, then rub off the skins in a clean dish cloth. Finely chop the nuts. Set aside half for decoration.

3 Lightly whisk the egg whites until foamy, then whisk in the salt and cream of tartar, and continue to whisk until they stand in stiff peaks.

4 Sift the sugar, flour, and cornstarch over the egg whites, add the almond and vanilla extracts, the dried blueberries, and half the chopped nuts, then fold in gently with a metal spoon until just combined.

5 Spoon the batter into the muffin cups, and bake for about 25 minutes, or until risen, pale biscuit-colored, and just firm to the touch. Transfer to a wire rack to cool.

6 To make the frosting, lightly whip the cream with the confectioner's sugar then whisk in the cream cheese until softly peaking. Spoon on top of the cupcakes and decorate with the reserved pistachio nuts and a few fresh or dried blueberries, if using.

makes 12

prep 25 mins
• cook 25 mins

12-cup
standard
muffin pan
• cupcake
liners

Cherry and coconut cupcakes

This classic combination of flavors is always popular. If you like, the cupcakes can be colored pink as well as the frosting.

INGREDIENTS

$^1/_2$ cup candied cherries
$^1/_2$ cup butter, softened
$^1/_2$ cup superfine sugar
2 eggs
$^3/_4$ cup self-rising flour
$^1/_2$ cup shredded coconut, plus extra for dusting
$1^1/_2$ tsp baking powder
few drops of pink food coloring (optional)

For the frosting

$^3/_4$ cup butter, softened
2 cups confectioner's sugar, sifted
4 tsp milk
few drops of pink food coloring
12 candied cherries

METHOD

1 Preheat the oven to 350°F (180°C). Line a cupcake pan with 12–15 paper liners. Wash, dry, and quarter the cherries.

2 Put the softened butter, sugar, eggs, flour, coconut, and baking powder in a large mixing bowl and beat well with an electric mixer for 2 minutes, or with a wooden spoon for about 3 minutes until light and fluffy. Add the quartered cherries and a few drops of pink food coloring (if using) and beat briefly again.

3 Spoon the batter into the muffin cups and bake for about 15 minutes, or until well risen and golden, and the centers spring back when lightly pressed. Transfer to a wire rack to cool.

4 For the frosting, beat the softened butter in a bowl. Gradually beat in the confectioner's sugar and milk until soft and fluffy. Beat in a few drops of pink food coloring. Pipe or swirl on top of the cupcakes, and top each with a dusting of shredded coconut and a candied cherry.

makes 12–15

prep 15 mins
• cook 15 mins

1 or 2 x 12-cup
standard
muffin pans
• cupcake liners

Coffee walnut cupcakes

This elegant cupcake makes for a sweet treat with morning coffee.

INGREDIENTS

$^3/_4$ cup walnut halves
$^1/_2$ cup butter, softened
$^1/_2$ cup superfine sugar
1 cup self-rising flour
$^1/_2$ tsp baking powder
2 eggs
2 tsp instant coffee granules, dissolved in 2 tsp hot water

For the coffee buttercream

1 tbsp instant coffee granules, dissolved in 1 tbsp water
$^3/_4$ cup butter, softened
2 cups confectioner's sugar, sifted

METHOD

1 Preheat the oven to 350°F (180°C). Line the cupcake pan(s) with 12–15 paper liners.

2 Reserve 12 walnut halves for decoration and finely chop the remainder. Place the softened butter, sugar, flour, baking powder, eggs, and the instant coffee solution in a large mixing bowl and beat well until light and fluffy. Fold in the chopped walnuts with a metal spoon.

3 Spoon the batter into the muffin cups and bake for about 15 minutes, or until well risen and golden, and the centers spring back when lightly pressed. Transfer to a wire rack to cool.

4 Meanwhile, make the buttercream. Place the instant coffee solution in a bowl. Beat in the softened butter and gradually add the sifted confectioner's sugar, beating until light and fluffy. Pipe or spoon the frosting on top of the cold cupcakes. Decorate each with one of the reserved walnut halves.

makes 12–15

prep 15 mins
• cook 15 mins

1 or 2 x 12-cup
standard muffin
pans
• cupcake liners

Vanilla cheesecake

This rich yet light cheesecake is guaranteed to be a crowd pleaser.

INGREDIENTS

4 tbsp butter, plus more for the pan
1½ cups crushed graham crackers
1 cup plus 1 tbsp sugar
1½lb (675g) cream cheese (not reduced fat)
   at room temperature
4 large eggs, separated
1 tsp pure vanilla extract
16oz container sour cream
kiwi fruit, thinly sliced, to garnish

METHOD

1 Preheat the oven to 350°F (180°C). Lightly butter the bottom and side of a 9in (23cm) springform pan.

2 To make the crust, melt the butter in a medium saucepan over medium heat. Add the graham cracker crumbs and 1 tbsp sugar and mix well. Press the crumbs into the bottom and 1in (2.5cm) up the sides of the springform pan.

3 Combine the cream cheese, egg yolks, ¾ cup of the sugar, and the vanilla in a bowl and mix with a wire whisk or an electric mixer on medium speed until smooth. In a separate bowl, using clean beaters, beat the egg whites until stiff. Fold the egg whites into the cream cheese mixture. Pour into the pan and smooth the top.

4 Bake for 45 minutes, or until the sides have risen and are beginning to brown. Transfer to a wire rack and let cool for 10 minutes.

5 Meanwhile, increase the oven temperature to 400°F (200°C). Whisk the sour cream and remaining ¼ cup sugar in a bowl. Pour over the cheesecake and smooth the top. Return the cheesecake to the oven and bake for 10 minutes more, until the topping looks set around the edges. Cool completely on a wire rack. Cover and refrigerate for at least 6 hours. Remove the sides of the pan, garnish with the kiwi fruit, and serve chilled, cutting the cheesecake with a wet knife.

serves 10–12

prep 20 mins,
plus standing
and chilling
• cook 55 mins

allow at least
6 hrs for
chilling

9in (23cm)
round
springform
cake pan

Strawberry cheesecake

This no-bake cheesecake takes very little time to make.

INGREDIENTS
3$^1/_2$oz (100g) bittersweet chocolate, chopped
3 tbsp butter
1$^1/_4$ cups graham cracker crumbs
9oz (250g) mascarpone
grated zest and juice of 2 limes
8oz (225g) strawberries
3 tbsp confectioner's sugar, plus more for sifting

METHOD
1 Melt the chocolate and butter in a small saucepan over low heat. Stir in the graham cracker crumbs. Press firmly and evenly into the springform pan.

2 Mash the mascarpone in a bowl with the lime zest and juice. Mix in the confectioner's sugar. Spread in the pan. Refrigerate for at least 1 hour to chill and set.

3 Arrange the strawberries over the cheesecake. Sift confectioner's sugar over the top. Remove the sides of the pan, slice into wedges, and serve chilled.

PREPARE AHEAD The cheesecake can be made up to 24 hours in advance, and chilled until required.

serves 8–10

prep 15 mins,
plus chilling

8in (20cm)
round
springform
baking
pan

Lemon poppy seed cheesecake with berry purée

This light alternative to cheesecake is especially good for a lunchtime dessert.

INGREDIENTS

2 lemons
10oz (300g) cottage cheese
10oz (300g) cream cheese, softened
1 cup sour cream
1 cup granulated sugar
3 tbsp cornstarch
4 large eggs, at room temperature
$1^1/_2$ tbsp poppy seeds
confectioner's sugar, for dusting
strawberries and raspberries, for garnish

For the purée

8oz (225g) hulled and sliced strawberries
$1/_3$ cup granulated sugar

METHOD

1 Preheat the oven to 300°F (150°C). Butter a 9in (23cm) springform pan. Grate the zest from the lemons and squeeze 4 tablespoons of lemon juice. Process the cottage cheese, cream cheese, sour cream, sugar, cornstarch, and 3 tablespoons of lemon juice in a food processor until smooth. Add the eggs and process to combine. Stir in the poppy seeds and transfer to the pan. Bake for $1^1/_2$ hours, or until the sides of the cheesecake are beginning to brown.

2 To make the berry sauce, purée the berries, sugar, and remaining 1 tablespoons lemon juice in a food processor. Cover and refrigerate.

3 Transfer the pan to a wire rack. Run a knife around the inside of the pan. Cool completely in the pan. Cover and refrigerate at least 5 hours, until chilled. Remove the sides of the pan, slice, and serve, with the berry purée.

serves 6–8

prep 20 mins,
plus chilling
• cook 1 hr 30 mins

allow at least
5 hours
for chilling

9in (23cm)
round
springform
baking pan
• food
processor

freeze for
up to 3 months

Blueberry-ripple cheesecake

The acidity of the blueberry fruit purée is the perfect foil for the smooth richness of this baked cheesecake.

INGREDIENTS

$4^1/_2$oz (125g) graham crackers
$1/_4$ cup butter
1 cup blueberries
$3/_4$ cup granulated sugar, plus 3 tbsp
12oz (350g) cream cheese, cut into pieces
1 cup mascarpone
2 large eggs, plus 1 large egg yolk
$1/_2$ tsp pure vanilla extract
2 tbsp all-purpose flour

METHOD

1 Preheat the oven to 350°F (180°C). Grease the cake pan. Put the biscuits in a food bag and crush with a rolling pin. Melt the butter in a saucepan, then add the biscuit crumbs and stir until moistened. Press an even layer of crumbs in the bottom of the pan.

2 Combine the blueberries and the 3 tablespoons of sugar in a food processor or blender and process until smooth, then push the mixture through a fine sieve into a small saucepan. Bring to a boil, then allow to bubble for 3–5 minutes or until thickened and jam-like. Set aside. Rinse the bowl of the food processor.

3 Combine the $3/_4$ cup sugar, the cream cheese, mascarpone, 2 eggs, vanilla, and flour in the food processor and process until well blended. Pour the mixture onto the crumb crust and smooth the top. With a teaspoon, carefully drizzle the blueberry mixture over the cream cheese mixture, swirling to make a decorative pattern. Bake the cheesecake for 40 minutes, or until it has set but still has a slight wobble in the middle when you shake the pan. Turn off the oven. Leave cake to cool in the oven for 1 hour, then cool completely in the refrigerator. Use a blunt knife to loosen the cake from the springform before unmolding to serve.

serves 8

prep 20 mins
• cook 40 mins

8in (20cm)
round
springform
cake pan
• food
processor
or blender

Baked stem ginger cheesecake

Fragrant ginger gives this cheesecake a new dimension.

INGREDIENTS

7oz (200g) package British digestive biscuits or plain cookies,
    such as gingersnaps, vanilla wafers, or graham crackers
2 tbsp butter
4 large eggs, at room temperature, separated
1 cup granulated sugar
6oz (175g) cream cheese, at room temperature
6oz (175g) mascarpone
2 tbsp syrup from a jar of stem ginger
4–5 pieces stem ginger, thinly sliced and cut into thin strips
2 tbsp all-purpose flour

METHOD

1 Preheat the oven to 350°F (180°C). Grease and line the bottom of an 8in (20cm) springform pan with parchment paper. Put the cookies in a plastic bag and crush with a rolling pin. Melt the butter in a saucepan, add the crumbs, and stir until evenly moistened. Spoon into the pan and press into the bottom to form a crust.

2 Put the egg yolks and sugar in a mixing bowl and beat with an electric mixer or wire whisk until thick and creamy. Stir in the cheeses, beat with a wooden spoon until smooth, and stir in the ginger syrup and sliced ginger. Sift in the flour and fold until no longer visible.

3 Put the egg whites in a bowl and beat until stiff peaks form. Fold into the yolk mixture, and spoon over the crust. Bake for 50 minutes, until golden and almost set. Turn off the oven and leave the cake inside to cool for 1 hour. Loosen the edges with a blunt knife and release the springform. Cover and refrigerate until serving time.

serves 6

prep 30 mins
• cook 50 mins

8in (20cm)
round
springform
baking pan

Black cherry cheesecake

This fresh cheesecake has a light texture and lemony taste, while the juicy cherries and syrup add a rich color and sweet flavor.

INGREDIENTS
6 tbsp butter
7oz (200g) graham crackers, crushed
1lb (450g) whole milk ricotta cheese
6 tbsp granulated sugar
grated zest and juice of 4 lemons
$^2/_3$ cup heavy whipping cream
$3^1/_2$ tsp unflavored gelatin

For the sauce
12–14oz (400g) can pitted dark sweet Bing cherries in
  syrup, or pitted dark tart cherries in light syrup

METHOD
1 Grease the cake pan and line with parchment paper. Melt the butter in a saucepan, add the biscuits, and stir until moistened. Transfer the mixture to the pan, pressing it down with the back of a spoon so it's level.

2 Mix the ricotta, sugar, and lemon zest together in a bowl. Put the cream in a bowl and beat lightly with an electric mixer or wire whisk until soft peaks form. Add to the ricotta mixture and beat with a wooden spoon until well combined.

3 Combine the lemon juice and gelatin in a small heatproof bowl, then place the bowl over a pan of simmering water and stir until the gelatin dissolves. Add to the ricotta mixture and fold in well. Pour the mixture on top of the crust, spreading it out evenly. Refrigerate for 2 hours or until set and firm.

4 Meanwhile, make the sauce. Drain the cherries, pouring the juice into a saucepan. Bring it to a boil, then allow to bubble for 10 minutes or until the juices have reduced by three-quarters. Leave to cool. Pile the cherries on top of the cheesecake, spoon on the sauce, and serve.

serves 6

prep 20 mins, plus chilling
• cook 10 mins

allow at least 2 hrs for chilling

8in (20cm) round springform baking pan

White chocolate cheesecake

The decadent white chocolate filling is coated with crisp dark chocolate.

INGREDIENTS

5$\frac{1}{2}$oz (150g) graham crackers
$\frac{1}{4}$ cup butter
7oz (200g) white chocolate
2$\frac{1}{4}$ cups ricotta cheese
2 large eggs
3$\frac{1}{2}$oz (100g) dark chocolate
4 tbsp heavy cream
fresh raspberries, to serve

METHOD

1 Preheat the oven to 325°F (170°C). Line an 8in (20cm) springform pan with parchment paper and grease the sides. Seal the graham crackers in a sturdy plastic bag, and crush with a rolling pin.

2 Melt the butter in a small saucepan and stir in the graham-cracker crumbs. Press evenly and firmly into the springform pan, smoothing over with the back of a wooden spoon. Chill in the refrigerator until needed.

3 Melt the white chocolate in a heatproof bowl set over a pan of barely simmering water, stirring occasionally. Beat the ricotta and eggs in another bowl until smooth, then mix in the melted white chocolate. Spoon the batter onto the graham-cracker base. Put the pan on a baking sheet. Bake for 45 minutes, until set. Remove the cheesecake from the oven and leave to cool in the pan.

4 When the cheesecake has cooled, release it from the pan and transfer to a serving plate. Melt the dark chocolate in a heatproof bowl set over a pan of barely simmering water, and stir in the cream. Spread the chocolate mixture evenly over the cheesecake. Chill for 2–3 hours, or preferably overnight. Scatter over the fresh raspberries, and serve.

serves 6

prep 25 mins,
plus chilling
• cook 45 mins

allow 2–3 hrs
for chilling,
or overnight
if possible

8in (20cm) round
springform
baking pan

Mini banana and chocolate cheesecakes

These chilled mini cheesecakes look and taste fabulous. Irresistible!

INGREDIENTS

4$\frac{1}{2}$oz (125g) shortbread cookies

2 tbsp unsalted butter

3$\frac{1}{2}$oz (100g) white chocolate, broken into pieces

1 cup cream cheese

2 large eggs, separated

$\frac{1}{2}$ cup heavy cream

$\frac{1}{2}$oz powdered gelatin

$\frac{1}{4}$ cup superfine sugar

2 bananas

juice of $\frac{1}{2}$ lemon

1$\frac{3}{4}$oz (50g) semisweet chocolate, grated, to decorate

METHOD

1 Line the muffin pan with 12 paper liners. Seal the shortbread cookies in a plastic bag and crush them with a rolling pin. Place the butter in a small saucepan over a gentle heat and stir until melted. Remove from the heat, add the cookie crumbs, and mix well. Divide the mix between the papers, press down firmly, then refrigerate for about 30 minutes.

2 Place the white chocolate in a small heatproof bowl, set it over a saucepan of simmering water, and stir occasionally until the chocolate has melted. Set aside.

3 Place the cream cheese, egg yolks, and cream in a large bowl, beat together until smooth, then stir in the melted white chocolate. Set aside.

4 Place 3 tablespoons of cold water in a small saucepan, sprinkle the gelatin over the water, and place over a gentle heat. Swirl the liquid around and stir constantly, making sure the water does not boil, until the gelatin has dissolved. Immediately remove the saucepan from the heat, and stir the gelatin into the cheesecake mix. Set aside.

5 Place the egg whites in a clean, dry glass or metal bowl and beat with a handheld electric mixer or a wire whisk until stiff peaks form. Continue whisking as you gradually incorporate the sugar. Fold the whisked egg whites into the cheesecake batter using a metal spoon. Divide the mix between the cupcake papers and refrigerate for at least 3 hours.

6 Once the cheesecakes are set, carefully remove them from the paper liners, loosening them first with a small knife. Finish by slicing the bananas and tossing them in the lemon juice to prevent them from browning. Make a circle of banana slices on top of each cheesecake, and sprinkle with grated chocolate.

PREPARE AHEAD The cheesecakes can be kept covered and in the paper cases without topping for up to 1 day in the refrigerator.

makes 12

prep 30 mins, plus chilling
• cook 10 mins

allow at least
3 hrs
for chilling

12-cup
standard
muffin pan
• cupcake
liners

MERINGUE CAKES

Lemon meringue roulade

A traditional filling is given a new twist in this impressive dessert.

INGREDIENTS

2 tsp cornstarch
5 large egg whites
$\frac{1}{2}$ tsp white wine vinegar
1 cup plus 2 tbsp sugar
$\frac{1}{2}$ tsp pure vanilla extract
1 cup heavy cream
1 cup lemon curd
confectioner's sugar, for sifting

METHOD

1 Preheat the oven to 350°F (180°C). Line a 10$\frac{1}{2}$ x 15$\frac{1}{2}$in (27 x 39cm) pan with parchment paper.

2 Dissolve the cornstarch in 2 tablespoons of water in a small bowl. Cook in microwave oven on high about 20 seconds, until boiling; set aside. Beat the egg whites and vinegar with an electric mixer until soft peaks form. Gradually beat in the sugar until the whites are stiff and shiny. Beat in the cornstarch mixture and vanilla.

3 Spread the mixture in the pan. Bake about 15 minutes, until lightly browned. Let cool on a wire rack.

4 Meanwhile, whip the cream until stiff. Fold in the lemon curd.

5 Unmold the meringue on another sheet of parchment paper. Spread with the lemon cream. Starting at a long side, roll up the meringue. Transfer to a serving platter. Cover and refrigerate until serving. Sift confectioner's sugar over the roulade and serve.

PREPARE AHEAD You can make the meringue up to a week in advance, and store it in a dry, airtight tin.

serves 8

prep 30 mins
• cook 15 mins

10½ x 15½in
(27 x 39 cm)
jelly roll pan
• electric
mixer

freeze for
up to 2 months

Apricot meringue roulade

The delicate flavor of apricots is intensified by adding passion fruit, whose wonderful perfume that makes this roulade very special.

INGREDIENTS

4 large egg whites
pinch of sea salt
1 cup plus 2 tbsp granulated sugar
$^{1}/_{4}$ cup sliced almonds
confectioner's (powdered) sugar, for dusting
1$^{1}/_{4}$ cups heavy whipping cream
15–16oz (400g) can apricot halves, drained
   and coarsely chopped
seeds and pulp from 2 passion fruit

METHOD

1 Preheat the oven to 375°F (190°C). Line a 13 x 9in (33 x 23cm) jelly roll pan with parchment paper. Combine the egg whites and salt in a bowl and beat with an electric mixer or wire whisk until soft peaks form. Beat in the granulated sugar 1 tablespoon at a time until the mixture is stiff and shiny. Use a spatula to spread it evenly in the pan. Scatter the almonds over the top, then bake for 15–20 minutes or until barely golden and just firm to the touch. Invert the meringue onto a sheet of parchment paper dusted with confectioner's sugar. Set aside to cool.

2 Place the cream in a bowl and beat with an electric mixer or wire whisk until soft peaks form. Spread the whipped cream over the meringue, then scatter the apricots and passion fruit seeds over the top. With the short side facing you, roll the cake into a cylinder and allow to cool to room temperature. To serve, dust with more confectioner's sugar and cut into slices.

serves 8

prep 30 mins
• cook 20 mins

13 x 9in
(33 x 23cm)
jelly roll pan

❄

freeze for
up to 2 months

Classic Pavlova

Both Australia and New Zealand claims to have invented this meringue and fruit dessert, named after the Russian ballerina Anna Pavlova.

INGREDIENTS
6 large egg whites, at room temperature
pinch of salt
1 tsp apple cider vinegar
1²/₃ cups sugar
2 tsp cornstarch

For the topping
1¹/₄ cups heavy cream
6oz (170g) strawberries, hulled and sliced
2 kiwi fruit, peeled and sliced
4 passion fruit, cut in half

METHOD
1 Preheat the oven to 350°F (180°C). Line a baking sheet with parchment paper. Beat the eggs and salt in a large bowl with an electric mixer or wire whisk until soft peaks form. One tablespoon at a time, add in the sugar and beat until the whites are stiff and shiny. Toward the end, beat in the cornstarch and apple cider vinegar.

2 Spoon the meringue onto the baking tray and spread into an 8in (20cm) round. Bake for 5 minutes. Reduce the oven temperature to 275°F (140°C) and bake about 1¹/₄ hours, until crisp. Let cool on the baking sheet.

3 Transfer the meringue to a serving platter. Whip the cream until it forms stiff peaks. Spread over the meringue. Top with the strawberries, kiwi fruit, and the passion fruit pulp. Serve immediately.

PREPARE AHEAD You can make the meringue base up to a week in advance, and store it in a dry, airtight tin.

serves 6

prep 15 mins
• cook 1 hr
20 mins

Rum and chocolate dacquoise

A dacquoise is made of crisp meringue disks layered with a filling. Serve it at a special meal.

INGREDIENTS

scant $1/2$ cup granulated sugar
scant $1/2$ cup dark brown sugar (packed)
3 large egg whites

For the filling

4oz (115g) semisweet chocolate, chopped
1 cup mascarpone
2 tbsp granulated sugar
$2/3$ cup heavy cream
$3/4$ cup toasted, skinned, and chopped hazelnuts
$1/2$ cup canned pitted black cherries, drained
3 tbsp dark rum
confectioner's sugar, to garnish

METHOD

1 Preheat the oven to 250°F (130°C). Draw three 7in (18cm) diameter circles on 2 pieces of parchment paper. Turn the papers upside down onto 2 baking sheets.

2 To make the meringue, mix the granulated and brown sugars together. Beat the egg whites in a bowl with an electric mixer or a wire whisk until soft peaks form. Gradually beat in the sugars until the meringue is stiff and shiny. Using a metal icing spatula, spread the meringue evenly within the circles. Bake about $1^1/2$ hours , or until crisp and dry. Cool completely.

3 To make the filling, melt the chocolate in a heatproof bowl over a saucepan of simmering water. Beat the mascarpone and sugar together, then mix in the chocolate.

4 Whip the cream just until it holds its shape and fold into the mascarpone mixture. Fold in the hazelnuts, cherries, and rum.

5 Place a meringue round on a serving platter and spread with half of the filling. Repeat with another meringue and the filling, then top with the final meringue. Refrigerate for at least 30 minutes. Sift confectioner's sugar over the dacquoise and serve.

serves 4–6

prep 30 mins,
plus chilling
• cook 1 hr
30 mins

Rhubarb and ginger meringue cake

Tart rhubarb and spicy ginger combine to make a tasty filling for this delicious meringue cake.

INGREDIENTS

For the meringues

4 large egg whites, at room temperature
pinch of salt
1 cup sugar

For the filling

1lb 5oz (700g) rhubarb, trimmed and sliced 1in (2.5cm) thick pieces
$^1/_2$ cup sugar
3 tbsp chopped crystalized ginger
$^1/_2$ tsp ground ginger
1 cup heavy cream
confectioner's sugar, for dusting

METHOD

1 Preheat the oven to 350°F (180°C). Line 2 baking sheets with parchment paper.

2 Beat the egg whites with an electric mixer or wire whisk until soft peaks form. One tablespoon at a time, beat in the sugar and the pinch of salt until the whites are stiff.

3 Spread the meringue on the baking sheets into two 7in (18cm) circles. Bake for 5 minutes. Reduce the oven temperature to 250°F (130°C) and bake for 1 hour, until crisp. Cool completely.

4 Meanwhile, cook the rhubarb, sugar, chopped ginger, ground ginger, and 2 tablespoons of water in a large covered saucepan over medium-low heat for 20 minutes, or until tender. Let cool. If too liquid, drain off some of the juices. Refrigerate for 2 hours.

5 Whip the cream until stiff peaks form and fold in the rhubarb. Spread 1 meringue with the rhubarb cream and top with the remaining meringue. Dust with confectioner's sugar and serve.

PREPARE AHEAD Make the meringues up to 1 week in advance; store in an airtight container.

serves 6–8

prep 30 mins
• cook 1 hr
25 mins

Mountain meringue cake

This is the perfect chewy dessert cake, especially if you have a sweet tooth.

INGREDIENTS

4 large egg whites

1 cup superfine sugar

$^2/_3$ cup pitted dried apricots, chopped

$^2/_3$ cup pitted dried dates, chopped

2 tsp cocoa powder

1 tsp instant coffee granules, dissolved in 1 tbsp boiling water

1 tsp cocoa powder, to decorate

1 tbsp sesame seeds, to decorate

For the nut buttercream

$1^3/_4$oz (50g) 70% dark chocolate

$^1/_4$ cup unsalted butter, softened

$^1/_2$ cup crunchy peanut butter

$^2/_3$ cup confectioner's sugar

METHOD

1 Preheat the oven to 375°F (190°C). Lightly oil the cake pans and line the base of each with a circle of parchment paper.

2 Place the egg whites in a large, clean, dry glass or metal bowl, and beat with a wire whisk or a handheld electric mixer until very stiff peaks form. Add the sugar, 1 tbsp at a time, beating until the mix is very thick and glossy peaks form. Fold in the apricots, dates, cocoa powder, and coffee solution with a metal spoon.

3 Divide the mix between the prepared cake pans and smooth to level. Place in the lower third of the oven and bake for 40 minutes, or until the meringues are golden and crispy on top. Remove from the oven and allow to cool completely in the pans.

4 When you are ready to assemble the cake, make the nut buttercream. Place the chocolate in a small heatproof bowl, set it over a saucepan of simmering water, and stir occasionally until the chocolate has melted. Place the butter, peanut butter, confectioner's sugar, and melted chocolate in a large bowl, and beat until the mix is thick and well blended.

5 Remove the meringues from the pans, place one meringue on a plate, and spread with the nut buttercream. Sandwich together with the second meringue. Decorate by dusting with cocoa powder, then sprinkle with sesame seeds. Refrigerate, covered, for several hours before serving, to allow the nut buttercream to harden slightly. Remove from the refrigerator about an hour before serving to bring the cake to room temperature.

PREPARE AHEAD The meringues can be kept, unfilled, in an airtight container for 1 day, but are best eaten the day they are made.

GOOD WITH Fresh fruit, such as raspberries or pears.

serves 8–10

prep 30 mins, plus assembling and chilling • cook 40 mins

allow several hours for chilling

two 8in (20cm) cake pans

freeze the meringues, unfilled, for up to 1 month

INDEX

Page numbers in *italics* indicate illustrations.

A

almonds
    Almond and orange cake 78, *79*
    Apple streusel cake *28*, 82, *83*
    Berry friands *26*, 154, *155*
    Cherry and almond cake 70, *71*
    Chocolate almond cake 60, *61*
    French almond financiers *25*, 148, *149*
    Orange and pistachio cake *27*, 74, *75*
    Panforte *132*, 133
    Raspberry cupcakes *176*, 177
    Raspberry, lemon, and almond bake 136, *137*
    Sticky lemon cake *27*, 68, *69*
    Stollen 110, *111*
angel cakes
    Angel food cake 36, *37*
    Blueberry and pistachio angel cupcakes
        20, 184, *185*
    Tropical angel cake *21*, *84*, 85
apples
    Apple fruitcake *21*, 86, *87*
    Apple muffins *22*, 160, *161*
    Apple streusel cake *28*, 82, *83*
    Cinnamon apple and raisin cupcakes 178, *179*
    Toffee apple bake *28*, 138, *139*
apricots
    Apricot cake *66*, 67
    Apricot crumble shortbread *26*, 134, *135*
    Apricot meringue roulade 212, *213*
    Mountain meringue cake *29*, *220*, 221

B

baking pans, choosing and preparing 7, *13*
baking powder 6
baking soda 6
bananas
    Banana bread 96, *97*
    Banana and chocolate chip muffins *22*, *158*, 159
    Banana, cranberry, and walnut loaf *26*, 104, *105*
    Mini banana and chocolate cheesecakes
        23, 206, *207*
    Toffee-topped banana cake *20*, 90, *91*
Bee sting cake (Bienenstich) *20*, 44, *45*
beets, Superfood loaf cake *27*, 108, *109*
berries
    Berry friands *26*, 154, *155*
    Lemon poppy seed cheesecake with berry purée
        196, *197*
    see also specific berries (eg raspberries)
Bienenstich *20*, 44, *45*
Black Forest gâteau *20*, 92, *93*
blondies, White chocolate and macadamia nut
    22, *116*, 117
blueberries
    Berry friands *26*, 154, *155*
    Blueberry muffins *24*, 162, *163*
    Blueberry and pistachio angel cupcakes
        20, 184, *185*
    Blueberry-ripple cheesecake *29*, 198, *199*
Brazil nuts, Toffee-topped banana cake *20*, 90, *91*
brownies
    Double chocolate 114, *115*
    Toffee 118, *119*
    White chocolate and macadamia nut blondies
        22, *116*, 117
butter 6
buttercream
    Cherry and coconut cupcakes *23*, 186, *187*
    Chocolate and buttercream Swiss roll *23*, 42, *43*
    Chocolate-frosted cupcakes 170, *171*
    Cinnamon apple and raisin cupcakes 178, *179*
    Coffee walnut cupcakes 188, *189*

Mountain meringue cake *29*, *220*, 221
Orange and lemon cupcakes *20*, *22*, 172, *173*
Petit fours *22*, 152, *153*
Rich vanilla buttercream frosting 18

C

candied fruit peel
    Florentine slices 130, *131*
    Panforte *132*, 133
    Stollen 110, *111*
carrots
    Almond and orange cake 78, *79*
    Whole wheat carrot cake *24*, 76, *77*
cheesecakes
    Baked stem ginger *29*, 200, *201*
    basic recipe and technique *14*
    Black cherry *25*, *29*, *202*, 203
    Blueberry-ripple *29*, 198, *199*
    Lemon poppy seed, with berry purée 196, *197*
    Mini banana and chocolate *23*, 206, *207*
    Strawberry *25*, *194*, 195
    Vanilla 192, *193*
    White chocolate 204, *205*
cherries
    Apple fruitcake *21*, 86, *87*
    Black cherry cheesecake *25*, *29*, *202*, 203
    Black Forest gâteau *20*, 92, *93*
    Cherry and almond cake 70, *71*
    Cherry and coconut cupcakes *23*, 186, *187*
    Cherry oat bars 128, *129*
    Rum and chocolate dacquoise *28*, 216, *217*
chocolate
    All-in-one chocolate cake with fudge frosting
        20, 46, 47
    Banana and chocolate chip muffins *22*, *158*, 159
    Black Forest gâteau *20*, 92, *93*
    Cherry oat bars 128, *129*
    Chocolate almond cake 60, *61*
    Chocolate Amaretti roulade *29*, 50, *51*
    Chocolate and buttercream Swiss roll *23*, 42, *43*
    Chocolate chip cupcakes 174, *175*
    Chocolate cookie torte *22*, *24*, 142, *143*
    Chocolate ganache 60, *61*
    Chocolate muffins *24*, 164, *165*
    Chocolate roulade *21*, 48, *49*
    Chocolate-frosted cupcakes *23*, 170, *171*
    Florentine slices 130, *131*
    Marble cake *26*, *54*, 55
    Mocha slice *28*, 126, *127*
    Mountain meringue cake *29*, *220*, 221
    Pear and chocolate cake *28*, *88*, 89
    preparation techniques *17*
    Rum and chocolate dacquoise *28*, 216, *217*
    Sachertorte *21*, 52, *53*
    Sticky toffee shortbread *22*, *124*, 125
    see also brownies; white chocolate
coconut
    Cherry and coconut cupcakes *23*, 186, *187*
    Coconut and lime cake *21*, *80*, 81
    Florentine slices 130, *131*
    Tropical angel cake *21*, *84*, 85
coffee
    Coffee walnut cupcakes 188, *189*
    Mocha slice *28*, 126, *127*
    Mountain meringue cake *29*, *220*, 221
    Nutty date muffins *24*, *150*, 151
    Pecan, coffee, and maple cake 56, *57*
cranberries, Banana, cranberry, and walnut loaf
    26, 104, *105*
cream, whipping and piping *16*
cream cheese
    frostings 76, 77, *80*, 81, 184, *185*
    see also cheesecakes
crème pâtissière 19

crumble shortbread, Apricot *26*, 134, *135*
cupcakes
    Blueberry and pistachio angel *20*, 184, *185*
    Cherry and coconut *23*, 186, *187*
    Chocolate chip 174, *175*
    Chocolate-frosted *23*, 170, *171*
    Cinnamon apple and raisin 178, *179*
    Coffee walnut 188, *189*
    Lime drizzle *27*, *180*, 181
    Orange and lemon *20*, *22*, 172, *173*
    Raspberry *176*, 177
    Strawberry and cream *22*, 182, *183*
    Vanilla *21*, 168, 169
curls, chocolate *17*

D

dacquoise, Rum and chocolate *28*, 216, *217*
dates
    Mountain meringue cake *29*, *220*, 221
    Nutty date muffins *24*, *150*, 151
    Sticky date bar cookies *23*, 122, *123*
    Tropical fruit and ginger cake *26*, 72, 73

E

eggs 6, *10–11*
equipment 7

F

figs, Panforte *132*, 133
financiers, French almond *25*, 148, *149*
flours 6
friands, Berry *26*, 154, *155*
frostings and icings
    chocolate fudge 46, 47
    chocolate ganache 60, *61*
    chocolate glaze 52, *53*, 174, *175*
    coffee *150*, 151
    coffee and maple 56, *57*
    cream cheese 76, *77*, *80*, 81, 184, *185*
    honey 44, *45*, 98, 99
    petit fours frosting 152, *153*
    piping technique *16*
    toffee 90, *91*
    see also buttercream
fruit cakes
    Apple fruitcake *21*, 86, *87*
    Caribbean tea bread 102, *103*
    Florentine slices 130, *131*
    Light fruitcake *26*, *64*, 65
    Stollen 110, *111*
    Superfood loaf cake *27*, 108, *109*
    Tropical fruit and ginger cake *26*, 72, 73
    see also specific fruits (eg lemons)

G

ganache, chocolate 60, *61*
ginger
    Baked stem ginger cheesecake *29*, 200, *201*
    Marmalade and ginger loaf *27*, 106, 107
    Rhubarb and ginger meringue cake
        29, 218, *219*
    Tropical fruit and ginger cake *26*, 72, 73

H

hazelnuts
    Panforte *132*, 133
    Rum and chocolate dacquoise *28*, 216, *217*
honey
    Honey cake *29*, 58, *59*
    Honey loaf *98*, 99
    Panforte *132*, 133

I

icings see frostings and icings
ingredients 6

mation

e equivalents

CELSIUS	DESCRIPTION
110°C	Cool
130°C	Cool
140°C	Very low
150°C	Very low
160°C	Low
180°C	Moderate
190°C	Moderately hot
200°C	Hot
220°C	Hot
230°C	Very hot
240°C	Very hot

uts

METRIC	IMPERIAL	METRIC
30ml	15fl oz	450ml
60ml	16fl oz	500ml
75ml	1 pint	600ml
100ml	1¼ pints	750ml
120ml	1½ pints	900ml
150ml	1¾ pints	1 liter
175ml	2 pints	1.2 liters
200ml	2½ pints	1.4 liters
240ml	2¾ pints	1.5 liters
300ml	3 pints	1.7 liters
350ml	3½ pints	2 liters
400ml	5¼ pints	3 liters

J
jelly rolls *see* roulades and jelly rolls

K
kiwi fruit
  Classic Pavlova *29*, 214, *215*
  Vanilla cheesecake 192, *193*

L
lemons
  Black cherry cheesecake *25, 29, 202*, 203
  Lemon, lime, and poppy seed cake
    26, 100, *101*
  Lemon meringue roulade 210, *211*
  Lemon poppy seed cheesecake with
    berry purée 196, *197*
  Lemon poppy seed muffins *24*, 156, *157*
  Orange and lemon cupcakes *20, 22, 172, 173*
  Raspberry, lemon, and almond
    bake 136, *137*
  Sticky lemon cake *27*, 68, *69*
limes
  Coconut and lime cake *21, 80*, 81
  Lemon, lime, and poppy seed cake
    26, 100, *101*
  Lime drizzle cupcakes *27, 180*, 181
  Strawberry cheesecake *25, 194*, 195
lining baking pans 13

M
macadamia nuts, White chocolate
  and macadamia nut blondies *22, 116*, 117
Madeira cake *32, 33*
Madeleines *22, 24, 146, 147*
mango
  Caribbean tea bread 102, *103*
  Tropical angel cake *21*, 84, *85*
  Tropical fruit and ginger cake *26, 72*, 73
maple syrup, Pecan, coffee, and maple
  cake 56, *57*
Marble cake *26, 54*, 55
Marmalade and ginger loaf *27, 106*, 107
mascarpone
  Baked stem ginger cheesecake
    29, 200, 201
  basic cheesecake recipe *14*
  Blueberry-ripple cheesecake *29, 198, 199*
  Rum and chocolate dacquoise *28, 216, 217*
  Strawberry cheesecake *25, 194*, 195
meringues
  Apricot meringue roulade *212, 213*
  Classic Pavlova *29*, 214, *215*
  Lemon meringue roulade 210, *211*
  Mountain meringue cake *29, 220*, 221
  Rhubarb and ginger meringue cake
    29, 218, 219
  Rum and chocolate dacquoise *28, 216, 217*
muffins
  Apple *22*, 160, *161*
  Banana and chocolate chip *22, 158*, 159
  Blueberry *24, 162, 163*
  Chocolate *24*, 164, *165*
  Lemon poppy seed *24*, 156, *157*
  Nutty date *24, 150*, 151

N
no-bake cakes
  basic cheesecake *14*
  Black cherry cheesecake *25, 29, 202*, 203
  Chocolate cookie torte *22, 24, 142, 143*
  Mini banana and chocolate cheesecakes
    23, 206, *207*
  Strawberry cheesecake *25, 194*, 195
nuts *see* specific types (eg almonds)

O
oats
  Cherry oat bars 128, *129*
  Oatmeal bars 120, *121*
  Sticky date bar cookies *23*, 122, *123*
oranges
  Almond and orange cake 78, *79*
  Orange and lemon cupcakes *20, 22, 172, 173*
  Orange and pistachio cake *27*, 74, *75*

P
Panforte *132*, 133
pans, choosing and preparing *7, 13*
paper liners 7
parchment paper 7
passion fruit
  Apricot meringue roulade *212*, 213
  Classic Pavlova *29*, 214, *215*
  Tropical angel cake *21*, 84, *85*
Pavlova, Classic *29*, 214, *215*
peanut butter, Mountain meringue cake
  29, 220, 221
Pear and chocolate cake *28*, 88, 89
pecans
  Apple muffins *22*, 160, *161*
  Pecan, coffee, and maple cake 56, *57*
  Toffee brownies 118, *119*
Petit fours *22*, 152, *153*
pineapple
  Caribbean tea bread 102, *103*
  Tropical angel cake *21*, 84, *85*
  Tropical fruit and ginger cake *26, 72*, 73
piping technique *16*
pistachio nuts
  Blueberry and pistachio angel cupcakes
    20, 184, 185
  Orange and pistachio cake *27*, 74, *75*
poppy seeds
  Lemon, lime, and poppy seed cake *26*, 100, *101*
  Lemon poppy seed cheesecake
    with berry purée 196, *197*
  Lemon poppy seed muffins *24*, 156, *157*
prunes
  Apple fruitcake *21*, 86, *87*
  Honey cake *29*, 58, *59*

R
raspberries
  Berry friands *26*, 154, *155*
  Raspberry cupcakes *176*, 177
  Raspberry, lemon, and almond bake 136, *137*
Rhubarb and ginger meringue cake *29, 218, 219*
ricotta cheese
  Black cherry cheesecake *25, 29, 202*, 203
  White chocolate cheesecake 204, *205*
roulades and jelly rolls
  Apricot meringue roulade *212*, 213
  Chocolate Amaretti roulade *29*, 50, *51*
  Chocolate and buttercream Swiss roll *23*, 42, *43*
  Chocolate roulade *21*, 48, *49*
  Lemon meringue roulade 210, *211*
  rolling technique *15*
  Swiss roll *24*, 40, *41*

S
Sachertorte *21*, 52, *53*
seeds
  Superfood loaf cake *27*, 108, *109*
  see also poppy seeds
separating eggs *10*
shortbread
  Apricot crumble shortbread *26*, 134, *135*
  Mocha slice *28*, 126, *127*
  Sticky toffee shortbread *22*, 124, 125

sponge cakes
  All-in-one chocolate cake with
    fudge frosting *20*, 46, 47
  basic recipe and technique *12*
  Bienenstich *20*, 44, *45*
  Chocolate almond cake 60, *61*
  Coconut and lime cake *21*, 80, *81*
  fruity *see* specific fruits (eg apricots)
  Honey cake *29*, 58, *59*
  Madeira cake *32, 33*
  Madeleines *22, 24, 146, 147*
  Marble cake *26, 54, 55*
  Pecan, coffee, and maple cake 56, *57*
  Petit fours *22*, 152, *153*
  Sachertorte *21*, 52, *53*
  Vanilla sponge 34, *35*
  Victoria sponge cake *27, 38, 39*
  White chocolate cakes *28, 140*, 141
  see also angel cakes; cupcakes;
    roulades and jelly rolls
Stollen 110, *111*
strawberries
  Classic Pavlova *29*, 214, *215*
  Strawberry cheesecake *25, 194*, 195
  Strawberry and cream cupcakes
    22, 182, 183
streusel cake, Apple *28, 82*, 83
sugars 6
Swiss roll *24*, 40, *41*
  Chocolate and buttercream *23*, 42, *43*

T
tea
  Caribbean tea bread 102, *103*
  Honey cake *29*, 58, *59*
techniques *10–17*
toffee
  Sticky toffee shortbread *22, 124, 125*
  Toffee apple bake *28, 138, 139*
  Toffee brownies 118, *119*
  Toffee-topped banana cake *20*, 90, *91*

V
vanilla
  Vanilla buttercream frosting 18
  Vanilla cheesecake 192, *193*
  Vanilla cupcakes *21, 168*, 169
  Vanilla sponge 34, *35*
Victoria sponge cake *27, 38, 39*

W
walnuts
  Banana bread 96, *97*
  Banana, cranberry, and walnut loaf
    26, 104, *105*
  Coffee walnut cupcakes 188, *189*
  Nutty date muffins *24, 150*, 151
  White chocolate cakes *28, 140*, 141
whipping cream *16*
whisking egg whites *11*
white chocolate
  Mini banana and chocolate cheesecakes
    23, 206, *207*
  Raspberry cupcakes *176*, 177
  Sticky toffee shortbread *22, 124, 125*
  White chocolate cakes *28, 140*, 141
  White chocolate cheesecake 204, *205*
  White chocolate and macadamia nut
    blondies *22, 116*, 117

Y
yeast-raised cakes
  Bienenstich *20*, 44, *45*
  Stollen 110, *111*

DORLING KINDERSLEY WOULD LIKE TO THANK THE FOLLOWING:

Photography
Carole Tuff, Tony Cambio, William Shaw, Stuart West, David Munns, David Murray,
Adrian Heapy, Nigel Gibson, Kieran Watson, Roddy Paine, Gavin Sawyer, Ian O'Leary,
Steve Baxter, Martin Brigdale, Francesco Guillamet, Jeff Kauck, William Reavell, Jon Whitaker

Recipe consultants
Peggy Fallon, Carolyn Humphries

Indexer
Susan Bosanko

And the following for work on additional recipes
Carolyn Humphries for the cupcake recipes; Yvonne Allison, Ah Har Ashley, Anna Guest, Mrs J Hough, Tracy McCue, Juliet
Montefiore, Catherine Parker, Jean Piercy, Emma Shibli, Penelope Tilston, Janet Wilson, and Galina Varese for recipe writing;
Hilary Mandleberg for recipe editing; Jane Milton and the recipe testers at Not Just Food; William Reavell for photography;
Jane Lawrie for food styling; Sue Rowlands for prop styling.

Useful infor

Oven temperatu

FAHRENHEIT

225°F

250°F

275°F

300°F

325°F

350°F

375°F

400°F

425°F

450°F

475°F

Volume equival

IMPERIAL

1fl oz

2fl oz

2½fl oz

3½fl oz

4fl oz

5fl oz (¼ pint)

6fl oz

7fl oz (⅓ pint)

8fl oz

10fl oz (½ pint)

12fl oz

14fl oz